# PROTECTION SPELLS

*A Comprehensive Beginner's Guide to Learn about Strong Protection Spells for Banishing Negativity and Ensuring Family Protection*

## JAMIE SALAZAR

# Table of Contents

# Introduction

Protection spells can help in numerous ways, especially if you want to find peace in the world or protect yourself from negativity. If you feel unsafe in a given situation or environment, it affects your emotional stability and health. This situation can also rob you of your mental strength and energy. The spells in this book can help you strengthen yourself mentally and physically. They give you a feeling of security and heal your mind and body.

Through spells, you can feel secure, protect your mental and physical wellbeing, and bask in calm and comfort. This feeling will help you be more relaxed. You will also find yourself living your life to the fullest. The spells in this book can also be extended to your loved ones.

Shielding and protective magic have three phases:

- Removal of negativity and malice if a psychological, psychic, or physical attack is threatened or has occurred.

- Protection from current attacks and future attacks.

- Restoration of good health, success, fortune, and harmony.

If you do not perform the third phase, you are going to have a vacuum in life. This void can be filled with low or negative energy. Therefore, you need to replace the energy you have removed. The spells in this book are protective and empowering. This book also focuses on protecting yourself from being affected by any negative energy and everyday nastiness.

If you are interested in defending your physical body and energy, then using spells is the best way to do this. If you have not worked with spells before, don't worry – this book is designed to help you understand the concept and practice different spells. Most spells in this book do not require anything more than creative visualization. You do not need to be an experienced or established practitioner to use the spells in the book.

This book is a quick guide to using defensive and protective magic. There are numerous ready-made spells in this book you can use. I hope you can use these examples to help you create your own spells. These spells can be associated with your goals and vision. You can also use your own ingredients and supplies.

# Chapter One

# Introduction to
# Working with Spells

Working with spells is called spell crafting. Spell crafting is the art of using the energy within and around you to regulate the energy in your world. Through spell crafting, you also can attune yourself to the different types of energies around you. Doing this will help you use those energies to your benefit. Don't forget that using spells is not a religious act. It is the method of using the energy around you to modify yourself and your surroundings. Using protection spells can help you reduce the stress you deal with regularly. Before we dive into what you can do with spells, let us understand what spells are.

## Introduction to Spells

A spell is a phrase or sentence said with some awareness and intent. This spell is aimed at creating change at a level. Spells only work because they are based on the principle that everything in the world is connected by energy. Before you perform any spell, you need to perform a series of symbolic actions. These actions are performed in the physical world so that you can activate or initiate some change on a different level. You can affect or change any situation through spells by redistributing or introducing energy within or around you.

You are the agent of any change you want to make in the world when you cast a spell. Any spell you cast focuses on different resources to direct the energy in the right direction. Your intent is to initialize change. Any consequences that occur because of the spell you use are your responsibility. Do not be like the witches on the Blair Witch Project. The girls began to use spells on people they did not like without worrying about the consequences. In the end, they were terribly affected by it because of the consequences of their actions.

Many people have tried to understand what the flowing life force means, and this concept has been explored in different parts of the world. This life force is called ka, qi, and prana in Egyptian religion, Chinese medicine, and Hindu philosophy. These terms are synonymous with the essence of any living being's existence. This powerful current of energy can animate every living being.

Like other divination and modern practices, spell work is based on the idea that the universe lies within every individual. Living beings represent the microcosm, while the universe represents the macrocosm. Spell work is the art of assessing, controlling, increasing, and focusing your energy on your intent. You don't have to use a book of spells or require any privileges to cast a spell. Most spellcasters use tools and ingredients in their spells to increase the effects, but the only thing you need to cast spells is your intent.

A spell is often performed with some intention. Incantations, on the other hand, are spells cast using phrases or words.

## What Do You Need for Protection Spells?

Every spell in this book has the items or ingredients you need to perform the spell. Most of these items are in your toolbox or cupboard. You do not require any special ingredients or items to cast any spell. You often only need yourself to be there. If you practice magic regularly, you may want to collect some antique items. These can be used during spell casting. Some spellcasters use candlesnuffers when they are performing magic, but you can use tongs instead of candlesnuffers to do this.

In this book, you will come across different candle colors and fragrances, but you can use generic ones if you prefer. Some generic fragrances are lavender, sandalwood, and rose. If you do not want to use fresh petals, you can use potpourri. Alternatively, you can use different flowers of the same color if you choose to stick to the colors mentioned in the book.

Most herbs that you need for spell casting can be found in the supermarket. Some herbs cannot be found at a local supermarket, so you would need to look for them in the local plant store. It is best to keep a box filled with different candles, candleholders, incense sticks, etc., should you want to cast spells on a whim.

You use candles to banish negative energy and offer protection or restore health, light, and fortune. The candles used in the former should be disposed of quickly, while the latter can be used to spread energy throughout the house even after you have cast the spell.

## What to Consider When Casting Spells

**Rules of Spellcasting**

Every thought and action behind a spell has a consequence on the universe and the people around you. Therefore, if you want to cast spells, ensure you do not mean harm to anybody around you. Most people may look at this differently, but ask yourself the following before you cast a spell:

1. Who should we not harm?

2. What does it mean to harm someone?

3. Is my spell going to focus on some people and cause harm?

4. Am I only looking to remove negativity from around me?

You need to be responsible for every action you perform and every spell you cast as a spellcaster. If you do not know what your actions can lead to, keep your intentions simple and clear. This is the only way you can safeguard the people around you.

**Do Not Use Manipulation as a Motive**

This is an important aspect to consider, and it is loosely based on the above. You may want to cast spells to change the way people around you behave. If you cast such spells, you will harm yourself and the person you are casting this spell on. You may also cause harm without actually meaning to if you do not have the right intentions when you start. Never use your spells to change how someone thinks, behaves, or acts. Do not try to influence their decisions.

There are times when you will find yourself in a relationship surrounded by the most toxic people, and it is important to learn to move on from them. It is also essential to understand why the person behaves the way they do. Help them understand the consequences of their actions. You can also wish for you or them to find realization and success away from each other. It is best to seek justice and not revenge. Trust that the universe will find a way to punish these people for treating you the way they do.

## Be Wary of Casting Spells for Others

You can use spells to protect yourself and the people around you, but it is important to be responsible when doing so. Do not cast spells for others unless you have spoken to them about it first. Never impose your practices and beliefs on people around you. In some cases, the person may come to you and ask for help. You can help them if you think you can. Do not use any spells without explaining to them how it will work and what they can expect.

## Maintain Privacy

I am sure you would have heard people telling you never to let others know what you wished for because it may not come true. Well, this is true when it comes to spellcasting. In the past, witches did not talk about their work because magic was believed to be evil. Most witches were burnt at stake or hung if their practices were revealed.

People now talk freely about their beliefs and practices, but people need to respect others. You cannot expect someone to have the same opinion as you, especially true for spiritual beliefs and practices.

Therefore, it is best never to tell people why you choose to cast a spell.

When you tell someone about what you want to do, their feelings about the practice may interfere directly or indirectly with your practice. Ensure you perform your magic in safe or private places. Within a circle or coven of trust, people can share their energy if they work towards the same intentions or goals.

**Protect Nature**

Never use harmful tools when you cast a spell. Ensure the material and ingredients used do not harm the environment. This will significantly reduce your negative impact on the planet. After each spell, you must clean up and dispose of some potions and mixtures. When you do this, be conscious about where you are throwing the waste. The best thing to do is to purchase ethically sourced or fair-trade ingredients. Purchase these ingredients from any local supplier. Alternatively, you can use your cooking skills to make your own potions.

**Ensure You Are Safe**

You will often use candles to perform spells, so ensure you use a sturdy holder when you perform the spell. Do not place candles next to any blinds or curtains in case they catch fire. If you leave a candle unattended, it can lead to trouble. If the candle must burn throughout the night, enclose it in a container or place it on a metal tray.

Apart from your physical safety, you should also focus on your mental health. A healthy mind thrives in a healthy body. If you experiment with essential oils, infusions, potions, or other products, ensure you are careful. Do not use magical solutions as a substitute for medicines because they will not help you take care of yourself. If you think you have a serious problem, you must speak to a physician or healthcare provider. Do not leave it to the universe.

## Protect and Cleanse Yourself

If you feel any energy blockages or disturbances when performing spells, you must regain your spiritual balance by performing a bath spell or spiritual cleansing. It is important to cleanse your mind and body. You should also cleanse personal spaces, such as your workplace, car, home, or any other place you frequent so that you can protect yourself from any negative energies or psychic attacks. You can prevent these regular interactions.

## Protecting Yourself before Spell Casting

The best way to dispel negative energy in any space is to use simple rituals. It is also important for you to protect yourself when you cast any spell, and the best way to do this is to cast a protection circle around you. This protective circle will allow you to work with lots of energy without causing harm to anybody outside the circle. It will also protect you from any negative energy from external influences.

Most spellcasters choose to create a protective spell around them by calling on the elements, cardinal direction, and energy. There is no need to cast a protective circle around you every time you cast a spell. Experts recommend you do this to add an extra level of protection around you. The protective circle also enables you to focus on your intent and cast the spell effectively. Use the protective circle to channel the right energy to manifest your intent clearly in the universe.

## Protection Circle

You can create a protection circle around you when you cast a spell, and this circle can either be big or small, depending on what you prefer. Some spellcasters believe this protective circle acts like a bubble. This bubble protects them and the people around them when they cast a spell. You can choose to draw a square, rectangle, star, or even a triangle if you do not like the idea of a circle. Your personal preferences, beliefs, and experiences determine how you choose to cast any spell. If you are an expert, you can simply visualize this protective circle around you.

## Steps to Cast the Circle of Protection

### Prepare the Tools and Altar

Once you cleanse the aura, prepare your altar and tools. If you do not have an altar, choose the spot where you will cast the spell.

If you have chosen to cast a spell in a room, ensure the area is clean. Negative energy in the room can affect the spell. The circle you cast your spell in should be pure. This circle is used to keep you and the people around you safe when you cast the spell. Clean the area using a broom or vacuum if you need to. Clean or purify the space using different crystals and objects. You can light incense or even play some soothing music to dispel the negative energy in the room. You can use salt water to clean the area as well.

If you want to use an altar, choose a flat surface, such as a table, as the altar when you perform the ritual. Alternatively, you can place a cloth on the floor in the center of the protective circle area. Ensure you are comfortable about where you are casting the spell. When you have the altar or area set up, you should represent the elements and directions. We will look at how you can do this in the next step.

**Invoke the Elements to Cast the Spell**

You will need to invoke the elements to infuse your spell with more energy when you cast any spell. You may also need to call on the divine spirit for some of these spells. We will look at how you can do this later in the book. Once you cast the circle, you should choose the directions and associate each direction with an element. It is best to stick to the standard mapping to ensure you do not go wrong or forget to invoke an element:

- Light some incense and leave it in the East end of your protective circle to invoke the air element.

- Since water is associated with the West, place a glass or bowl of water in the West.

- Invoke the fire element to the South. You can do this with a white candle. This candle symbolizes the element and can add an extra layer of protection.

- The earth element is associated with the North. So, leave a bowl of salt in the area of the circle associated with this element

After you do this, you should call on the divine spirit to guide you through the spell casting. Say, "I ask the Divine spirit to bless this circle. Within it, I am free and protected. So, this shall be."

You can change the words to suit your spell casting methods. Once you invoke the Divine spirit, begin the spell. You can also perform this activity after you draw the protective circle around you.

**Draw the Circle**

You can either use an athame or a wand to draw the protective circle around you. Follow the steps given below to draw the circle:

1. Before you cast the circle, take a deep breath, and relax. Visualize the protective energy in your body and observe how it builds when you breathe.

2. Now, focus on your breath, and use your intent and willpower, directing the energy from your inner self to your dominant hand and arm.

3. Focus on the wand or athame and feel the energy flowing from your arm into this object.

4. Visualize the energy flowing as a stream from the tool and settling as a layer on the ground.

5. Now, draw the circle using the tool numerous times to strengthen the protective circle.

Visualize the circle around you. Regardless of the method you use to draw this circle, you must visualize how the circle protects you from negative energies. If you do not want to use a tool, you can resort to using the index finger of your dominant hand.

## Understand How Much Space You Need to Cast Any Spell

Cast a big protective circle around you. You should be able to move freely within this circle when casting spells. Ensure you can extend your arms and legs as far as you can within this circle. If you want to move around the circle or stand in the center of the circle while you perform the ritual, create a bigger circle. Visualize this area and draw the circle using a tool. Alternatively, you can demarcate the area using crystals or tools, such as ropes, sand, or candles. If you are wary of using certain objects, stick to drawing the circle using a tool or your index finger.

## Complete the Ritual and Open the Circle

On completing the ritual or spell, you should open the circle. To do this, hold your wand and athame in your hand. Move these in opposite directions to neutralize the power of the protective circle. You can also say the following words: "Thank you for your energy. I am now opening this protective circle." You can change the words if you want to. Thank and honor the spirits and nature since you used the energy from them to cast your spell. After you do this, leave the circle. Do not blow out the candles if you have used them to cast the spell.

**Extra Tips**

- The protective circle is your vault of energy, and the strength of this circle depends on your visualization and focus. Use meditation to help you focus and calm yourself before you begin casting this circle around you.

- Ensure you have everything you need to cast the spell before you begin creating the protective circle.

- Once you finish casting the spell, remember to close the circle. Do not let any energy from outside the circle influence or change what you have done in the protective circle

## How Does the Protective Circle Help?

A protective circle is a barrier between the energy within you and the world outside. It protects you from any negative influence, such as destructive energy or distractions. These can disrupt your focus and will make it harder for you to cast the spell and manifest your intent in the universe.

Most spellcasters cast spells at home or in their rooms. If someone were to open a window or door while you cast a spell, they give the energy a chance to flow from you. If you have a protective circle around you, it becomes easier to contain the energy. This circle can also be used to prevent interference from any other spellcaster.

If you are worried about spell casting, and this is normal, use the protective circle to create a bubble around you. You can work with different spells and ingredients to see what works best for you. When you are inside this circle, you will not be affecting anybody else.

Having said that, you should watch your words. If you want to break the circle or barrier, carefully walk out of it and dismiss it. This is a very important step, and you should do this if you want to complete the ritual.

People often use spells and magic to protect themselves or their loved ones from spiritual, mental, or physical harm. They can also use spells to attract love, wealth, happiness, and more. If you use white magic spells, you will use positive energy to cast the spell. This would mean the consequences of the outcome are pure and clear. If you use black magic, you are going to pay for what you have done.

White magic spells improve your life, but it is important to stick to the rules so you do not affect anybody through your spells. Do not stop yourself from trying something new when it comes to spellcasting. The only thing you should focus on is your environment and body. Cleanse them frequently so your thoughts and intentions remain pure.

It is best to draw a protective circle around you and the altar when you cast a spell. This will prevent the energy from moving out of the circle. Another thing you need to do is to learn how to cast a spell and choose the right words when you cast the spell. Your intent should be pure, so it can manifest in the universe, thereby helping you achieve your desired outcome.

There are two functions to this magic circle:

1. To protect the energy you have gathered to cast the spell.

2. To protect you and your loved ones from any harm.

You need to contain all the energy for the spell only in this circle. Once you finish casting the spell, let the energy out of the circle and move to the universe.

Most spellcasters do not create a protective circle using the above method. Some do not cast a protective circle at all. Experts recommend you do this so negative energy does not enter the circle and affect your spell. You can try different methods to cast this circle and find the method that suits your needs best.

## Tips for Successful Spellcasting

You may not be confident about how you cast a spell, and it will be difficult for you to train your mind. If there is a change or shift in your thought or mindset, the spell can backfire, which will have detrimental effects on you and the person you have cast a spell on. Use the tips below to remain confident during spell casting.

### Secret #1: Trust the Spell Will Work

If you constantly worry about whether or not your spell will work, you are only making it harder to focus on the intent. This worry is negative energy, and it can have a detrimental effect on the outcome of your spell. Do not constantly worry about messing up. Focus only on your intent and see what you can do to improve.

Trust the spell you have written and have faith the universe will work in your favor. Any negativity is counterproductive. If you catch yourself worrying about the outcome of a spell, snap out of it and focus on your intent. The magic will work, and you should avoid disturbing it. Give the universe some time to work on your intent so that you achieve the desired results.

**Secret #2: Stop Worrying about the Tiny Details**

You may have found yourself in a situation where you did not find the ingredients you needed to cast the spell. The substitute you chose did not work as well as you would have wanted. I am sure you may have read a million articles before you began casting spells, and all the information out there may have started to worry you. Let me tell you something – the tiny details do not matter. Magic is only about your intent. Your steps and actions do not affect your intent. So, why should you worry?

The substitutes you use may not align with your intentions, but it may work in your favor if you focus all your thoughts and energy on the substitute. It is tricky to substitute herbs or oils in complex spells, and you may not learn what works for you until you tinker with it. So, do not worry if you want to work with different ingredients, just practice and identify one that suits your spell the best. You can change the elements if you believe the energy in them does not resonate with your beliefs.

It is okay to forget a few words of the spell or stammer when you cast a spell. This does not mean your spell will not work. Some spellcasters stammer and stutter, and this is a problem they have. This does not stop them from casting spells, so why should it stop you? You may find it hard to complete an incantation, but do not let frustration and anger seep in because they will affect the outcome of your spell.

It is important to accept that you are going to make mistakes when you cast a spell. Understand that as long as your intentions are pure, you will not cause harm to yourself or anybody when you cast the spell. If you focus on your energy and intent the entire time, the spell will work even if you do not say the right words. Your intent manifests in the universe. Do not tire your mind by worrying about the tiny details or errors. Perfection is not what you should strive for when you cast a spell. Do not let imperfect casting make you feel you cannot get it right.

**Secret #3: Understand You Need Time to Focus**

You cannot expect your spiritual side to kick in and the energy to flow the minute you decide to cast a spell. For example, you may find it difficult to relax and go on vacation, especially after a stressful time at work. This happens because your mind is focused on work and needs some time to switch to vacation mode. The same can be said about your transition to the spiritual mode. When we try to skip from one activity to another, we often deny ourselves the necessary space to switch into our witch mode.

The skills you learn and develop in school and work cannot help you with spell casting. People believe they can behave like machines, but they fail to understand that their mind is not built this way. Your mind can switch from one task to the next in a matter of seconds, but you need to focus on what task you want to do if you want to do it right. You also need to give yourself time. So, if you choose to cast a spell after work, give yourself enough time to switch from your work mode to your spiritual mode. Give yourself enough time so you can make the transition before you cast the spell.

Most spellcasters have trouble when it comes to making this transition. Also, they are probably impatient. If you feel the same way, you can create a ritual. This ritual should be easier for you to dive into the process. The next chapter has some rituals you can use to make it easier to focus. Perform these rituals before you cast a spell.

The ritual can either be simple or elaborate, depending on the type of person you are. You can take a bath or meditate for a few minutes before you cast a spell. No matter what you choose as your ritual, ensure you practice it enough so that it becomes the best way for you to focus your intent before you cast any spell. This ritual will enable you to switch to the right mindset before you begin the casting. It will take some time to implement this ritual, so give yourself enough space and time, so you can get into the right mindset to cast a spell.

**Secret #4: Use Theatrics as Often as You Can**

Most people choose to cast spells for personal reasons, and the conventional methods are quite boring. The best way to make the process interesting is to use theatrics and a little drama. This process is where you use theatrics to make the process more fun! You can dress up, put on some music, create a witchy ambiance, and get into character. Do not worry about the outcome of your spell as long as your intent is clear and strong. It is about setting the stage so you can get into the right mindset. Create an environment where you feel witchy. You can do what Professor Trelawney does in Harry Potter. Use a different voice if you want to like her.

Yes, this does sound a little dramatic and fake, but once you know how to do it, you will see why you need this to cast a spell. Theatrics set the right mood and help you focus on the goal or objective. You can use these theatrics to find the energy you need to cast a spell. Most spellcasters choose theatrics since it gives them confidence.

When you find yourself in character and in an environment where you can cast a spell, you will lose yourself. It becomes easier for you to achieve your goals in this mindset and environment. If you choose to cast spells, you do not have to stick to the regular methods or ideas, but do what makes you feel best when you cast spells. Spellcasting does not have to be a tedious task, so make it as fun as you want. You can use different elements and methods to set the right mood before you cast a spell.

## Types of Magic Spells

### Love Spells

There are numerous spells one can cast to change how someone sees you. You can also cast a spell to motivate a person to fall in love with you. Spells can also be cast to strengthen or improve a relationship, revive love between two people and reconcile with your loved one. Love spells can be used to forget people who hurt you or prevent any affairs. Love spells can be used in different ways, as long as they do not cause any harm to people.

You can write a spell to address any issue you face. Once you cast the spell, wait for it to take effect. It is best to use white magic when you cast love spells since these do not cause any harm. Ensure you have the right intent and understand your feelings so you do not negatively affect yourself or your target.

**Wealth or Fortune Spells**

Of course, you would love to boost your luck. Anybody would. You may also want to improve your financial status. Anything is possible with spell casting. Wealth and fortune spells have numerous variations, such as attracting more money, winning the lottery, eliminating debt, getting extra work in money, or more. You may find yourself running out of money, but these spells can change your destiny.

You not only must cast spells but can also define your own rituals to remove any negative energy from your surrounding environment and within yourself. It is best to clear your aura through sacred baths, and you can perform this ritual at least three times every month to attract prosperity. This will increase your luck at home and work.

**Health Spells**

If you feel unwell often, you can cast spells to help you feel better. If you do not know the spell you should cast, speak to a professional spellcaster and they will use powerful health spells to improve your condition. All they need to know is the problem you are facing and they will come up with a solution to remove the negative energy and eliminate any pain or aches. They can heal your aura with quick spells too. Do not miss these spells since they improve your physical being a lot.

## White Magic Spells

White magic is harmless magic but very powerful. If you want to lead a life filled with happiness and harmony, use white magic spells. As mentioned earlier, spellcasters choose to perform any ritual or cast spells using white magic. They know this is the best way to obtain peace, harmony, and safety in your life. But what is white magic? This magic is innocent, and the objective is to protect and help vulnerable people. Through white magic spells, you can gain everything good in the world without harming or destroying those around you.

When you perform different spells and rituals using white magic, you can combat different problems in life. You can restore the balance of peace and harmony in your life while protecting yourself from any negative energy around you. Any spellcaster who uses white magic will first explain the situation to you and help you understand what white magic is. These spells remove any bad habits and negativity. Using these spells also helps you overcome emotional pain.

## Black Magic

Black magic is the opposite of white magic. Using black magic, you can fulfill every intent or want of yours without worrying about the consequences. You will not worry about the ethics of magic when you perform a black magic spell. With these spells, you can get anything you want and protect yourself from any hexes or curses. I would recommend you do not use black magic in any situation except for a protection spell. Do not cast these spells on your own as well.

Black magic spells are difficult to perform. Magic is very sensitive, and you may not know its power, especially as a beginner. So, do not take black magic lightly or even use it.

# Chapter Two

## Rituals and Practices

If you are a beginner, here are some points to keep in mind as you practice. Start small. Try to incorporate some of the rituals mentioned in this section into your routine. Before you cast a spell, you need to perform a ritual to cleanse yourself and focus on the intent. You can use one of these rituals to help you focus and improve your spell work.

### Use a Candle and Focus on the Flame

Most spellcasters choose to light candles, using the flame to calm themselves down and focus on the intent. Light a candle when waking in the morning, when brushing your teeth, or even getting ready for work. Alternatively, you can light a candle on your desk at school or work or even before you go to bed. The flame creates a sense of calm and soothes your mind.

### Use a Crystal and Absorb the Energy

The best way to connect with different tools is to energize them and focus on their properties. Crystals are used in most spells, and it is easier to use the energy in crystals to help you focus. All you need to do is hold the crystal in your hands and focus on its energy. If you want to purchase a crystal, hold it for a few minutes and focus on the energy in the crystal. If you find yourself resonating with the energy, you can purchase the crystal. You can also meditate to connect with the energy in the crystal. Once you select your crystal, place it under your pillow or wear it anywhere on your body.

## Stir Your Drink in a Counterclockwise Direction

If you drink either tea or coffee in the mornings, it is best to stir the drink in the counterclockwise direction using a spoon. This helps to remove negativity from your day.

## Focus on Your Breathing

It is easy for people to lose their focus when they cast spells, especially if it's hard for them to do so. You can use different methods to focus on your breathing, and the best way to do this is to perform Surya namaskar by following the steps given below:

- Take a deep breath and exhale while you join your palms at the heart center.

- Take another deep breath and raise your hands above your head.

- Exhale and slowly bend forward. Make sure to keep your knees straight and try to touch your toes. If you are flexible, you can also move your forehead closer to the knees.

- Take another breath and shift your hands so your fingers touch the floor in front of your toes. Lift your head and look forward.

- Exhale and bend your head towards your knees.

- Take another deep breath and slowly raise your body and lift your arms above your head.

- Exhale and bring your hands to your heart's center.

Perform this exercise at least ten times every day at home.

## Use Oil Rollers

If essential oils calm you, carry a glass bottle filled with the oil of your choice. Ensure the bottle has a rollerball since this piece of equipment can be used to relax your muscles. This is a handy piece of equipment to keep in your purse or at your desk. If you need to focus or require a pick-me-up, apply a little oil behind your ears and on your wrists. Inhale the aroma as you use the roller.

## Drink Tea

It is a good idea to drink tea when you are working on being mindful and keeping yourself calm. Make herbal tea if you want to. Heat the water and watch the tea brew, inhale the aroma, and focus only on your breath to calm your mind. Sip the tea slowly to calm your insides, as well.

# Chapter Three

# Steps to Casting Magic Spells

## Set Up an Altar

You do not necessarily need an altar to perform a ritual or cast a spell, but having one is beneficial. Some spellcasters choose not to have altars but don't have a problem with casting their spells. A few spellcasters use their tables or any other surface at home to cast spells. They use a clean, white cloth to cover the surface before they cast the spell. Some choose to sit on the floor instead.

If you look for spells online, you will be asked to sit at an altar before you cast a spell. Why do you think this is important? Before you perform any magic, you need to create a sacred space for yourself to manifest your intent using magic.

## Preparing the Bath

You need to cleanse yourself of any negative energy before you cast spells, and the best way to remove the energy is to take a ritual bath. This enables you to prepare yourself physically and mentally before you cast the spell or perform rituals. A daily shower does not keep your body fresh and clean, and for this reason, you need to use a ritual bath to calm your body and mind. Not every magic circle will ask you to begin with casting a protection circle, but it is best to draw one around you before you cast spells. This will prevent the entry or movement of bad or negative energy from around you into the circle. You can also prepare yourself mentally through a ritual bath.

## Defining Your Motives and Intentions

As mentioned earlier, your intentions are very important when it comes to casting spells. You need to know what your intent is and what your end goal is. It is important to be specific when you work with energies. Do not be general because it can add some confusion to the spell. Avoid using negative phrases, sentences, and words in your spell.

You should have good intentions when you cast a spell. Your intent should not affect anybody and should be for your happiness. Having said that, you should understand that spells you cast will affect those around you, so ensure your spell does not harm anybody around you. Only when your thoughts and intentions are pure can your spell work. There can be no negativity in your mind when you cast the spell.

To do this, write your intentions and thoughts down on a piece of paper or in your spiritual journal. This is a great way to frame your desires and use the right words when you cast a spell. As you write it down, you should describe your innermost desire with meaningful and clear words. This will help you understand your wants and needs better. Do not use the phrase 'I want' when you send messages through a spell. It is best to say you are grateful for everything you have.

## Lighting Candles

Most spells you cast require the use of candles. If you do choose one such spell, you should light it only when you have determined and worded your intent. Place this candle on the altar before you light it. When you do this, it indicates to the universe you are ready to change some aspect of your life. In the realm of magic, a candle is used because it has a connection to the spiritual world.

Different parts of the candle represent different elements in the universe:

- The wax is associated with nature and represents the earth element.

- The hot wax dripping and melting on the side of the candle represents the water element.

- The smoke is associated with the air element.

- Lastly, the flame is associated with purity and represents the fire element.

It is both enlightening and beneficial to use candles when you perform any ritual. Candles not only refresh your mood and change your mindset but also enhance the power of the spell you want to cast. The color of the candle and its flame will attract different types of energies depending on the type of spell you want to cast and your intent. Candles have healing powers and are the main ingredient in any spell you cast, and the color you choose depends on your intent and circumstance.

## Meditating before You Cast the Spell

This is an important part of any spell casting ritual. You should focus on your intent before you begin the spell. The best way to do this is through meditation.

Before you meditate, you need to empty your mind so you can focus only on your intent. This is important if you want your spell to work. According to an experienced spellcaster, meditation is very important if you want to cast spells. You cannot expect the spell to work simply because you use an altar, place all the ingredients on the altar, and pray with candles. The most important aspect is to concentrate on your objective or intent before you cast a spell. In the next section, we will look at how you can control your thoughts through meditation.

When you perform a spell, you should focus on your goal. This intent and focus will transform into energy. So, don't be doubtful or afraid of what may happen. You also should rid yourself of any negative emotions. The energy you put out into the universe will be scattered and weak before the session ends if you let negativity seep in.

## Make or Chant a Prayer

Once you focus on your intents, visualize, and meditate, cast the spell. Chant the words you have written down by saying a few words.

When you do this, you can send your message to the universe. All you need to do then is to trust the universe will grant your wish. As mentioned earlier, be very specific about your intent if you want the spell to work for you.

Once you are done with the spell, thank the universe for listening to what you must say.

# Chapter Four

# Basics of Meditation

Most people have trouble controlling their emotions and thoughts when they cast spells, and this often lets some negative energy seep into the spell. You may find it difficult to focus on your intent because you worry about every small detail in your life. This only affects your mental and physical health, making it hard for you to focus on the spell you are casting.

One of the easiest ways to focus more and worry less when you cast spells is to meditate. When you meditate, you allow yourself to be open to all of your thoughts and emotions and learn to stop judging them. This is the only way for you to let go of the negativity in your life. If you have just started with meditation, you cannot meditate for longer than a few minutes. You will improve if you continue to stick to this routine.

When it comes to meditation, you should keep a few things in mind.

## Choosing When to Meditate

If you want to start meditating, you should commit to the practice. Start small. Meditate a few times a week. You need to ensure your schedule allows you to meditate. Spend at least ten minutes every week meditating. You also need to find a place for yourself where you will not be disturbed. It is okay to have background sounds. You need to persevere and discipline yourself when you begin a new habit. Therefore, it will also take time for you to honor a routine.

Ensure you stick to the same routine every day. It is only this way that you can improve your practice. Most people meditate around the same time they perform another routine habit. This will make it easier for them to remember to meditate. The mornings are the best time to meditate, but it is okay for you to meditate any time during the day. Do not meditate at night since your body will associate it with sleeping.

## Clothing

Your clothing does not matter when it comes to meditation, so wear anything you feel comfortable in. The important thing is for you to be relaxed and comfortable. If you are wearing a belt, scarf, or tie, loosen it before you meditate. Remove any uncomfortable heels or shoes. If you want, you can meditate wearing nothing if you are in the privacy of your own home.

## Duration

Your schedule and preference determine how much time you spend on meditation. It is important to meditate frequently. The duration is not as important as the frequency. When you start with meditation, begin with a short session. Stick to five or ten minutes. If it is easy for you to meditate for this long, increase the duration by 5 minutes. You should do this until you train your mind. It is hard for most people to sit in silence for longer than ten minutes, so you need to meditate for 3 or 5 minutes if you feel this way. Give this a shot and then slowly build your confidence as it grows.

**Position**

Since you can meditate whenever you want, you can either meditate inside or outside the house. You can sit on a cushion, the floor, a chair, or a bench. Make sure you sit in a position you are comfortable in. Unless you *want* to sit down in a cross-legged position, you do not have to. You can forgo stereotypes if they don't resonate with you. If you are a beginner, you should sit straight when you are trying to familiarize yourself with the practice. Sit down on a cushion or chair and keep your back straight. Tuck your chin slightly in and relax your neck. Rest your hands on your knees or lap.

**Take It Slow**

The process of meditation is tricky. You cannot expect to succeed on your first attempt. Even experts took years to master this skill. Take it slow. Focus on your schedule and choose to meditate at least once every day. The practice of meditation requires patience, practice, and commitment. You will feel the benefit over time. There is no bad or good meditation. This also indicates you cannot expect to succeed or fail at meditation. There is only non-awareness and awareness or non-distraction or distraction. When you learn to control your distractions, you become more aware.

## Know Your Motivation

People often meditate to focus on their intent. This practice will make it easier for you to focus on your intent when you cast spells. Your motivation can either be specific or broad. The motivation can be different for everybody. It is, however, important to start with the right motivation. You should know why you want to meditate. If you have a good idea about why you want to meditate, you will stick to the practice. You can create the right mindset and focus on the spell when you are certain about your intention.

## Stay Mindful After Meditation

Most people meditate because they want to be aware of how they feel in the present moment. If you want to use meditation to help you focus, you should recognize how your thoughts and emotions affect your focus. Commit to carrying these thoughts with you for the rest of the day. It is also important for you to determine what you want to do next, whether it is making breakfast, brushing your teeth, shower or taking a walk. You may lose your calm easily after a round of meditation, but do not let this happen. Focus on your intentions and thoughts. Carry your emotions with you throughout the day and focus on the tasks at hand.

# Chapter Five

# Magic and the
# Law of Attraction

It is important to understand that the law of attraction is not a random theory but an important phenomenon in your life. It is also important for you to understand this law if you want to cast spells. Magic focuses on the use of this law. Whether the one who casts the spell realizes it or not, the strength and success of their spell rely, to a large extent, on the law of attraction. The significance of this law is evident when you achieve the result. This spell can be used to compare the effects of two spells on you.

The base of the law of attraction is very simple - 'like attracts like' and 'think about something hard enough, and the universe will provide.' These may seem like lines straight out of a motivational book or speech, but this doesn't weaken the truth. Like does attract like, and the energy you put out there will manifest in the universe. The more complex explanation would be the universe is responsive to your thoughts and emotions. If these emotions are strong enough, then it will find a way to align things so they play out your way.

Essentially, if you are keen on a certain outcome and truly believe the outcome is possible, the outcome will come to fruition. Let us say you leave your house in the morning under the impression that you will have a good day, then everything happening during the day will most likely be a good experience. In fact, your mind may even gloss over the bad things that happened just to prove how good your day was. This is exactly how you thought your day would be like. The same can be said about waking up and believing you have a bad day.

It is difficult to understand this concept if you are a beginner, but the law of attraction is simple. Everything that happens to you now is a result of positive thoughts you had about a situation at some point. Through your experiences, you will understand everything that has happened to you is because of a thought or intent you put out into the universe. You will also understand, with time, these outcomes are based on your thoughts and beliefs.

It is because of your thoughts and emotions that you brought those situations upon yourself. The law of attraction is an experience that is best learned through observation and practice. Having said that, your affinity for magic will certainly ensure you understand the law faster than most people will.

## Practicing the Law of Attraction

It may take you some time to understand the law of attraction so it will take you some time to begin to use it in your practice. You need to train your mind well so that you can use the law of attraction the right way. Using some exercises, you can learn to focus on the outcome you want to achieve. You can also determine when you want to achieve this outcome.

You can break this thought process down as follows:

1.  Appreciation

2.  Affirmation

3.  Visualization

When you focus on all three aspects together you can obtain the desired outcome. Let us understand these terms better.

## Appreciation

Appreciation is related to gratitude. It is crucial to acknowledge the facts when things are going rather well for you in the present. When you do this, you force yourself to become more aware of everything happening around you, the good and the bad. This is the only way you will know what works best for you. When you accept and acknowledge all the good things, you become more receptive and aware of the positivity around you. This also means you do not focus on any negative thoughts and emotions, making it easier for you when you cast spells.

## Affirmation

An affirmation is one where you validate everything you have appreciated. You need to repeat the outcomes of each day, preferably only the positive ones, so you become more aware of the good things around you. Having said that, you must also be ready to reaffirm yourself when things do not go according to plan. When you do this, you can give yourself the information you need to pick yourself back up. This may seem like you are trying to fake it until you make it. Many agree that this type of positive outlook and self-motivation can make it easier for you to reach new heights.

**Visualization**

Visualization is the easiest one because we have all visualized something at some point in our lives. You may have dreamed about protecting yourself and your loved ones. You may also have dreamed about your ideal life, fortunate situations, and a great house. These images are only present in your mind because your imagination runs wild. When channeled along with appreciation and affirmation, visualization can also be a powerful tool.

Additionally, you should also train yourself to experience the feelings associated with achieving this dream. When you visualize these feelings of triumph and victory, you can use the law of attraction to your benefit and attract all the good things. The law of attraction works in its primary form when one has mastered the art of using these three skills together. Coordinating in this way strengthens your magic.

Spell work is built on the combination of appreciation, affirmation, and visualization. When they are combined, you can harness enough energy to manifest your desire. Visualization allows you to understand what is expected, appreciation brings you closer to reality, and affirmation rounds off the deal by having you say the spoken word. This spoken word will seal the deal for the enchantment. This is evident from simple spells like lighting a candle all the way up to more complex procedures.

If magic is the art of using energy to bring about the desired effect, then these three things are the tools required to channel the energy effectively. The law of attraction is often the best way for you to understand the basics of magic.

## Getting Started With Making Spells

It is difficult for you to create or write your own spell, but do not let this stop you. The only ingredient you need to cast the spell is the intention, and any object you use while you cast the spell should first be charged energetically. You must not purchase any healing crystal if you want to cast any spell. Black pepper, cayenne pepper, cinnamon, and sugar are the best spices to use when you cast spells. You can also use these spices when you prepare potions, infusions, or oils. You can use cooking pots to prepare these potions.

Don't forget that once you use an object in a spell, you have repurposed the objective of the object. This object will now be magical. This means a wine glass used to prepare a magical potion cannot be used to serve wine to guests. If your spell focuses on entertaining guests, then you can do this. Every tool you use to cast spells is going to contain energy, so ensure you maintain a record of the objects you use.

Creating and writing spells will empower you. This process can be fun so enjoy yourself.

**What Should One Know About Making Spells?**

It is difficult to make spells if you are a beginner. Some experienced spellcasters also find it difficult to make spells, and this may leave you feeling anxious. You should be confident about what you want to do and practice as often as you can. In this section, we will look at some points to remember before you make or cast spells.

**Preparing Ingredients**

Some spells do require specific ingredients or objects to strengthen the power of the spell. This does not mean you must spend a lot of money buying the necessary objects for spell casting. You can use something as simple as a pebble or stone. You can energize this instead of buying a healing crystal. If you cast a spell at home, you can use different ingredients from your pantry, such as herbs, honey, and paper. Some herbs you can use include black pepper, cinnamon, and other spices. You can also use essential oils depending on what you need for the spell. You can use a candle to enhance the power of any spell you cast.

If you want to use potions before you cast spells, purchase cauldrons. Use your cooking skills to your advantage. It is important to remember that the object becomes magical once you choose and use it when you cast spells. Some tools have a lot of energy in them, and therefore, you should clean them regularly to ensure the energy in them is pure.

**Choosing the Location**

When you are looking for a place to cast your spells, ensure you choose a room with a window or doorway. A doorsill or windowsill is termed a cosmic entrance. This indicates it can be used to create a connection between the spiritual and physical world. This is the perfect way for you to connect with the cosmos.

So, before you cast your spells, choose the best location for the process. If you want to increase your chances of success, cast your spell when night and day intersect. You can also cast these spells during important times of the year. The only thing to remember is to choose the right place to work on your spell and cast it. Ensure you close every door or window around you before you perform the ritual.

The most important thing for you to do is to keep your intentions clean and pure. Do not try to harm someone through your spells.

# Chapter Six

# Using Crystals to Cast Spells

Crystals are often used in spell casting, and you need to choose the right one for you to ensure the spells have the desired effect. Before you choose a crystal, you need to determine if you resonate with its energy. Use your intuition to help you choose a crystal. In this chapter, we will cover some crystals and their benefits in spell casting. We will also look at how they can be used to balance energies.

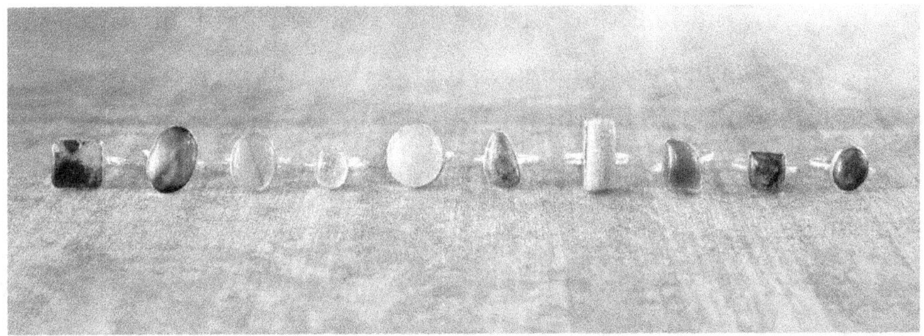

## Clear Quartz

This is one of the best crystals you can use to heal and balance the energies in your body. This crystal does not have a negative effect on you, but you would need to cleanse the crystal in sunlight before you use it. This crystal makes it easier for you to clear all types of energy in your body, thereby making it easy for you to strike a balance. Use this crystal before you cast a spell to cleanse your body and mind. You can also use it to help you focus on your intent.

**Onyx**

Everybody has the yin and yang energies in their body. These are opposing forces of energy, and an imbalance can affect you mentally and physically. When you cast a spell, it is important to balance these energies so you do not cause any harm to the people around you or even to yourself. The crystal helps you focus on the good things in life, thereby filling you with positive energy.

**Peridot**

Peridot is a crystal used to inspire yourself. This crystal will strengthen you and cleanse the energy in your body. You can also use this stone to protect yourself or your loved one from any harm. The stone rids any anger, fear, jealousy, or worry you may have before you cast a spell.

## Amethyst

Amethyst can convert any negative energy in your body to positive energy. The energy in this crystal flows freely through your body, especially your subconscious. It becomes easier for you to access the meditative state while you heal, and this is because it works well with your third eye chakra. You can use this crystal while you meditate. You can use this crystal to focus on your intent when you cast a spell.

**Pyrite**

Spellcasters use pyrite to remove negative energy from their mind and body. This stone makes it easier to quell negative thoughts before you cast a spell, so your intentions are pure and harmless. You will become optimistic and trust the process.

**Rhodonite**

Spellcasters often use this crystal to boost their confidence before they cast a spell. Most spellcasters are worried about their spells and the outcomes of those spells. Even the slightest negative energy during spell casting can have damaging effects on the person you are casting this spell on. Therefore, it is important to train your mind to focus only on the intent. You can use this stone or carry it on your person while you prepare yourself to cast the spell. The energy from this stone will make it easier for you to focus on the outcome alone before you cast the spell.

**Lapis Lazuli**

Spellcasters use Lapis Lazuli to clear the mind of any negative thoughts and emotions before casting a spell. It becomes easier to calm your mind and focus on the intent when you are casting a spell. Hold this stone in your hand if you are unsure of casting a spell or find yourself having trouble focusing on the intent. Feel the energy from the stone coursing through you. You will find your thoughts flowing freely and can use the energy from the stone to protect yourself from making any hasty decisions.

Experts recommend you place this crystal near your third eye chakra. This chakra is present in the center of your forehead. This crystal will make it easier for you to open your mind to absorb the right energy. Since this crystal is also called the dream catcher, it becomes easier to focus on your intent when you cast a spell.

**Tourmaline**

Tourmaline is commonly termed the protection stone since this can create a protective shield around your body and mind to ward off any negativity. Some protection spells use this stone, and we will look at one such spell later in the book. The crystal can be used to visualize a protective shield around you or your home. You would, however, need to carry this crystal on your person once you cast the protective spell.

## Hematite

Hematite is used to train your mind to focus. This crystal removes any negative energy and thoughts in your mind before you cast a spell. Negative thoughts and emotions have damaging effects on any spell you cast. Since magic is based only on your intent, it is important to ensure this intent is not tainted with negative energy. In the form of negative feelings, emotions, and thoughts, this negative energy will make it hard for you to focus on your outcome and goal.

Using this crystal makes it easier for you to rid yourself of any inhibitions. This will give you confidence in your spell casting techniques. You will also stop questioning your abilities and will appear confident while you cast a spell. If you use this crystal along with clear quartz, you can balance your thoughts and emotions.

## Moonstone

Moonstone spreads a sense of calm in the person holding it. Women often keep this stone on their person during their pregnancy to keep them calm. The crystal's energy is balanced. The crystal can help you focus on your thoughts and calm yourself down before you cast a spell. Your focus will sharpen when you use this crystal while you cast spells. This crystal can also be used to balance the energies in your body. It becomes easy to keep all your negative emotions at bay.

**Tiger's Eye**

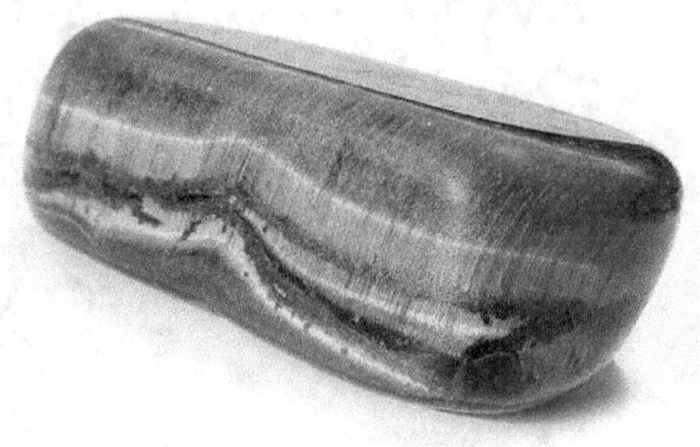

Spellcasters often use the tiger's eye to boost their confidence, so they cast a spell without any obstacles. Most spellcasters, especially beginners, worry about casting spells and focus on your worry instead of the intent. Using this crystal before casting the spell makes it easier for the spellcaster to focus and take charge of the situation.

The crystal also gives you the strength to protect yourself from any negative thoughts or threats. The energy from the crystal works with your adrenaline glands. The energy will neutralize any fear or negative energy in the glands, thereby helping you think coherently.

## Smokey Quartz

Spellcasters often use Smokey quartz to absorb any negative energy around them caused by pain and suffering. This crystal can neutralize the feelings of pain and ground the energies in your body. This indicates the earth absorbs all the negative energy. You can use this stone to help you focus on your positive energy before you cast a spell. The crystal helps to spread a sense of calm throughout your body, thereby removing any obstacles when you cast a spell.

**Rose Quartz**

This crystal is associated with love. This crystal works best when used with your heart chakra. If you want to use a binding spell on a loved one, you can use this crystal by placing it close to your heart chakra. The crystal will balance the energy in your heart chakra and throughout your body. This will make it easier for you to look at the positive side of things. This crystal also helps with overcoming grief and depression since it balances the energies in your body. This energy will make it easier for you to focus on yourself and love every aspect of yourself. Any resentment you feel towards the people around you will vanish when you use this crystal. It is best to use this crystal before you perform any spell to get rid of negative thoughts.

**Agate**

Agate is a strong stone, and you can use it to give yourself confidence give you the courage you need to perform a spell. If you do not want to cast a protection spell but want to have conversations with the people hurting you, you can use this crystal to strengthen your mind and body. If you use this stone, you will perceive the environment around you in a positive light. Since the crystal is also known for its grounding capabilities, it will cleanse your energy and leave you feeling better at the end of the spell. The crystal also helps to ground you and leave you with immense energy. The best part about this crystal is the energies in your body, and both the yin and yang can be balanced easily using the energy in this crystal. This enables you to use the energy to the best of your abilities.

# Chapter Seven

# What Is the
# Law of Manifestation?

As mentioned earlier, you need to believe you have achieved everything you need or want, and when you look at it this way, you can manifest your intent. So, why do you need to learn about the law of manifestation?

The Law of Manifestation, also known as the law of beamed energy, is one of those laws used to facilitate the Law of Attraction. You can use these laws to strike a balance between the energies present in the universe. Otherwise, there will be chaos.

Having said that, you know there cannot be order in the world if there is no chaos. This also works the other way round, meaning if there is no order in the world, then there would only be chaos. It is important to ensure the energies in the world are balanced so that there is harmony and peace in the world. Negative energies in the world cancel each other out, thereby bringing a semblance of balance in the universe.

Of the different laws governing the energies and their balance in the universe, the law of manifestation is most important. According to this law, you can achieve anything if you know what you want. The only thing you need to do is to manifest or let the universe know your intent. If you want to make this law work for you, create an image of what you most desire and fix this image in your mind. The trick is to focus on what you want and not what you think you need. It is also important to ensure your desires do not cause an imbalance in the universe.

It is easy to work with materialistic things since you know what to create in your visualization. If you wish to live in a mansion, you can easily create this image in your mind. When you fixate and focus all your energy on this image, your intent manifests in the universe, and you will achieve it. It is difficult when you must create an image of your desires, especially those with an emotional aspect tied to them. For this reason, spell casting is hard. It is difficult to create an image when it comes to relationships, or revenge, or even the death of a person.

## The Law of Manifestation

Everybody has desires, and this goes for you too. You need more and want more because you discover new things about yourself. Once you have identified your desire, focus on what you must do to achieve it. It is also a good idea to focus on how you would feel once you achieve your desire. The thought and immense devotion to your desire are what help it manifest itself into the universe.

Once you are sure of your desire, you can indicate to the universe in clear terms. When you do this, the universe works hard to ensure you achieve what you most desire. As mentioned before, a desire for a material object can manifest itself easily in the universe. It is the desires with an emotional connection to them that are difficult to.

All your desires are located deep in your subconscious, and when you are calm you remember these desires. Once you identify this desire, focus on it, and think of it every free second you get. This way, you can manifest that desire in the physical and spiritual world. This is the only way the universe takes notice of your desires. It will then work hard to ensure you achieve everything you need.

Einstein was a master at understanding energy. He believed human beings could create energy through their thoughts. These thoughts could produce large volumes of energy, and this could be used for different purposes. A perfect example of one such character is Charles Xavier from X-Men. He could project his thoughts and communicate with the people around him through thoughts because of the energy associated with those thoughts.

There are many reasons to justify that visualization is the best way to manifest your desire in the mind's eye. You might confuse visualization with daydreaming, but this is not true. Visualization is a process, and you need to understand this process to ensure your desires manifest in the universe.

Through visualization, you can manifest your desire or want in your mind's eye. You should do this consciously and deliberately. You need to focus all your energy on this desire alone. If you have read Harry Potter, you can associate this with the process of Apparition. Or, if you know Nightcrawler from X-Men, visualization is like what he does. Nightcrawler, along with witches and wizards in Harry Potter, focuses on the destination he wants to move to. This energy enables them to move to the place. Nightcrawler never goes wrong because his intent is clear. He knows exactly where he has to go and has the image in his mind. Apparition, on the other hand, is slightly tricky.

Through Apparition, a wizard can move from one location to another simply by focusing on the destination. When he has perfect concentration and focuses all his energy on the image in his mind, he will reach the destination safely. If the same wizard was distracted and thought of a million places at once, it would negate all his images of the initial destination. He might not be able to reach his destination safely. He must practice discipline to avoid dying because of Apparition.

In the same way, you must clearly picture what you desire most. This image must be visualized and detailed perfectly to help the universe understand what it needs to do to help you achieve your desire. You must pour all your energy into your desire to ensure that your subconscious takes in all the information and helps manifest the desire in the universe.

There are two aspects of Visualization. The first is to create the image of what you desire in your mind. This image needs to be detailed. This detailing is what helps the universe understand what you desire or want most. The second aspect is to assume that what you desire has already been given to you. When you identify these two aspects and use them, you will find that it is easy to achieve whatever you desire. This is because your desire becomes a thought that manifests itself into either the spiritual or physical world.

While performing this process, you must ensure that you have mental, physical, and visual discipline. Only when you have a great deal of discipline will you receive what you desire most. You must have steadfast faith that you will achieve what you most desire. Even a tiny negative thought can hinder your results. As mentioned above, the universe works on the notion that a balance of energies exists in the world. When you wish for something and let negativity creep in, you will realize that the energies cancel each other out. This cancellation of energies leads to an alteration in the results. Therefore, you must possess a certain level of discipline.

It is known that when you focus on your desires regularly, they manifest themselves faster in the spiritual or physical world. You must use the methods mentioned below to ensure that your desire manifests itself. When you perform these exercises, your subconscious is in a state to receive any message from you or the universe. It will accept your desire and the visualization of that desire and helps manifest that vision into the spiritual or physical world.

You can use different techniques to ensure your dreams and desires manifest themselves in the universe. Once you have created your desires and dreams, your subconscious sends the dream out into the spiritual or physical world. The next section tells you how you can ensure that your desires have manifested. These methods follow the Law of Manifestation.

**Simple Vision**

This method is a simple way to ensure that your desire manifests in the spiritual or physical world. To use this method, follow the steps below:

1. Take a few deep breaths and calm your mind and body. Do this using meditation or other breathing techniques. You must keep yourself calm and happy. If you cannot do this, listen to soothing music.

2. Focus on what you most desire. Focus on the intent and why you need to achieve that goal. Once you do this, add some details to the intent. This should be done the way a sculptor details his sculptures.

3. When you visualize the intent, focus on your higher consciousness, and ensure you pull all the energy you need to cast the spell. Visualize your image moving to the point between your eyebrows. This is the place where your third eye is located. Now assume that your third eye is sending this image out into the spiritual world or the physical world.

4. Visualize that your favorite mode of transport is doing this – it could be a horse or even your favorite car. It is here that your desire manifests itself.

Using this method, it becomes easier for you to send a message to the universe and let it know what you want from the spell you cast.

## Magical Ritual

You might have your own place of worship at home. If you have cast spells before, you can use the altar. Once you have identified your desire, you must identify objects associated with this desire. Now, place the object on the altar. If you have the desire to get engaged to the one you love, use the engagement ring you have purchased for the person or use an object representing the person.

If you desire something else along with the engagement, job, or house, ensure you have objects to represent it. For example, you can have a check for the house from your dream company or a miniature house. Once you do this, write four or five lines to describe the intent or desire. Use simple words to do this.

Once you do this, calm yourself. You can do this through mediation. If this does not help, listen to soothing music, and calm your mind. As mentioned above, you must visualize your dream. Keep your desire in focus and try focusing all the energy you possess on the dream. Then light a candle at the altar and recite the lines you have written about your desire. Ensure you pour all your intent into these lines. Call on your favorite Deity, and then prepare yourself for the spell work.

Keep the image of your desire in your mind's eye. Ensure this image is as detailed as possible. Now, hold this object in your hand and state clearly to the universe that the object represents your energy. It is important to understand that the object also holds your creative energy.

The energy you put into your visualization should move into the object. Imagine the energy is flowing into the object from your subconscious mind. Once you are ready, recite the statements you have written down on a piece of paper. Now, place the object back on the altar and light a candle. The candle enhances the energy of your desire. Repeat the lines again. You must believe the light from the candle is heavenly and is helping you manifest your dream. You must be honored and thank the deity you have called upon.

Before you use any of these methods to manifest your intents, emotions, and thoughts into the universe, learn to journal. Write down what your intentions are and how you want to go about achieving them. Note all the changes you perceive in your life when you focus on your intent and work towards achieving it.

Before you cast any spell, you must visualize your intent, and you can do this using one of the methods discussed earlier. Once you have chosen your method of manifestation, you must record what you have done – the exact method. You should make sure you note every detail without fail. If you have done anything extra for you to achieve your dream, you must mention this too. Once your desire does manifest, you must record the events that occurred. You must remember to be eternally grateful to the deity you have called upon to assist you.

## Fire Method

When you use the fire method, you need to follow the steps you did for simple vision. If you want this method to work the right way, you should first focus on yourself and learn to calm down. You need to keep yourself calm and happy.

If you find you cannot calm yourself down easily, meditate or listen to soothing music. Use the tips mentioned earlier in the book if you want to meditate. You must then visualize what you want most. Once you have identified your desire, picture it in great detail. This must be done in the same way an architect details the designs of a building or a museum. Write all these details down on a piece of paper. This will help you remember your desire and the details of the desire with ease.

Another way to focus on your intent is to detail it. Focus your energy on this intent and its details. Then dig into your subconscious and give your desire all the energy you possess within yourself. Make yourself believe that what you have created as your desire has branded itself into your subconscious.

Now place the paper inside a glass bowl or a glass container. Light the paper on fire. Associate the flames with the energy you possess within your spirit. Once you have focused all the energy onto the flame, set the paper on fire. Visualize the smoke and associate it with the smoke released from the back of a vehicle carrying your dream to the universe.

The dream will now manifest in the spiritual and physical world. However, this depends on whether you desire material things or your desire is tied to emotion. Your intention determines how soon the desire manifests in the universe, and this is like how a spell works.

Keep these steps in mind so you can cast the spell and achieve the desired results.

It does become very difficult to create the right image in your head when it comes to casting spells. You may not know how to focus only on your intent, but you will not find it hard to do this if you practice. When you know what you want, it becomes easier for you to identify what you should do to achieve that dream.

It becomes easier to determine the amount of spiritual and physical energy you should put into the spell to achieve the desired result. When you understand this, you will learn to manifest your intents and thoughts.

The methods mentioned in this chapter are simple and can be used even by beginners. Magic is not complicated, and it only focuses on the transfer of energy. You must, however, identify a method that works perfectly for you. The method you choose to cast the spell or manifest your intent is the only way you can achieve your goal.

Using these methods, you can manifest your intents and thoughts into the spiritual and physical world, making it easier for you to cast your spells and reap the benefits. You need to understand what the law means and how you can use it. Then you can use any spell, or the methods mentioned in this chapter, to help you manifest your intent.

# Chapter Eight

# A Guide to Protection Spells

Now that you have an idea about a simple protection spell, let us look at what you would need to do to cast the right spells.

## Create a Spiritual Plan

If you are dealing with any problem or issue in life or want to achieve something in life, you can use spells to do this. This does not mean a spell can solve all your problems. For this reason, every spellcaster practices magic carefully and thinks twice before choosing a spell or technique.

A spiritual plan includes the following:

- An intent or thought behind the goal or the situation you want to protect yourself from.

- Focus on how any action, magical or non-magical, will affect you and your loved ones. Understand the consequences of your actions.

- Choose your friends and loved ones wisely to create a support system around you so that you can rely on others for help.

- You can look at situations from different perspectives and see whether your reaction is reasonable.

- Request for help from the divine spirit to aid you in everything you need to do.

This may seem difficult for any beginner, especially if the spells are complicated. If you learn and understand what spell casting is and how you can do it, you can increase your chances of succeeding.

**The Energy You Need to Get Rid of and the Energy to Keep**

Magic is a representation of any actions you can perform to activate or reject any universal energy. If you remove negative energies and focus on positive ones, you can protect yourself from all harm. Every spellcaster performs two types of magic – banishing and manifesting. The former means you are removing something, while the latter means making or creating something new.

**The First Steps**

The first step to protecting yourself and a loved one is to focus on controlling how you approach life itself. You need to change the way you look at yourself. If you think you are a loser, you are going to continue to visualize yourself in this way. Choose to look at yourself as the winner.

Every protection spell you perform relates to common sense, mood, and emotions. This indicates that you should never be reckless when it comes to casting protection spells. Do not cast a spell if you are drunk or angry. This will change the outcome of the spell. The universe may help you protect yourself or your loved ones, but if you are not careful about your intentions when you cast the spell, you may cause more harm than good.

The most important rule is to never rely on black magic to perform any protection spell. Different things may be happening to you. You may want to change the outcome of a specific situation, but it is best not to use black magic to do this. Instead, ask the divine spirit to help you cast the spell. When you use the help of the spirit, you will see what the universe is trying to say to you.

Why do you think you should do this? Let us assume there is a fire in your house. What would you do in such a situation? Would you use water to douse the fire or use fire to combat fire? Black magic is synonymous with the latter. When you use black magic, you invite more negative energy into your life. It is important to combat any situation by being open.

If you have done something wrong, expect the universe to do something to teach you a lesson. We all need this reminder at some point in life. Learn to correct yourself and focus on what is most important for you. Do not focus on improving a situation simply because you believe it should be done this way.

**Avoid the Dark Side**

If you are intelligent, you know not to use magic to harm anybody. You do this because you know negative energy does not help you overcome different situations. People choose to use black magic only because they believe people who practice white magic are weak because their magic does not help them obtain the desired results.

If you choose to use black magic, pause and think again. The world has both chaos and order, and when there is a balance between the two, you can live in peace and harmony. You need both of these energies for the world to exist. This does not mean one is evil and the other is good. If you do want to cast spells, ensure you only use white magic.

You should defend yourself when someone harms you. There are various times in life when you may find yourself angry at how things are going for you. In such situations, it is best to avoid using black magic since you will only harm your chances of protecting yourself or your loved one. Instead of using negative energy to channel your thoughts and intentions, you should learn to banish it.

**Does It Take Long to Cast a Spell?**

You can complete casting a protection spell in a matter of minutes or months. Before you perform any protection spell, you need to perform a ritual to cleanse your mind of any negative thoughts. It is best to choose one ritual and master it. For instance, if you want to protect yourself or a loved one, you can write a spell in a matter of minutes. You may take only a few minutes to cast a spell to create protective barriers for your loved ones. If you want to help someone with a more difficult problem, you may take longer. A spell may not work immediately, so do not let this affect you. Work on this spell again. You should recast this spell as often as you can. The activity is complex, so it will take time for the magic to take effect.

If you choose to cast a spell regularly, you must practice this spell before you cast it. You cannot make silly mistakes while casting this spell since they can lead to grave consequences.

## When Should You Cast a Protection Spell?

Most witches use the moon phase to identify the period they are in to perform the spell and reap the benefits. While there are eight phases of the moon, most spellcasters work with the following:

1. Black moon – to banish

2. Full moon – to gain power

3. Waning moon –to rebuild and rework

4. New moon – to focus on something new and important

5. Crescent moon – to build

How long do you need to wait before you can see the effects of the spell on yourself or your loved ones? You need to wait until the spell takes effect, and this is for the following reasons:

1. Magic will only work if you focus on your intentions and thoughts. If any of your thoughts affect the power of magic, it will take longer for the magic to manifest. If you add more

hurdles when you cast a spell, you will affect the manifestation of your intent. You should, therefore, be clear about what you expect from the spell.

2. It is best to start with small goals since the effects of magic appear faster. For instance, if you spread some salt around the house, it will absorb the negative energy and improve the situation in your house. Some issues may take longer than others, so give yourself some time

3. If you have difficult objectives to work with, you may need to strengthen the spells you want to cast. You may need to use different spells or magic every week for you to achieve the objective. If you cast spells with too many people in mind, it is going to take longer for the magic to take effect

You should forget about a spell once you have cast it. If you have negative thoughts while you cast spells, the objective of the spell will weaken and the manifestation will take longer. If you focus only on the outcomes, you will create roadblocks, which will make it difficult to cast the spell. You need to be sincere about your intention.

**Does Every Ingredient Need to be Present When I Cast a Spell?**

Any spell you cast is based on certain energies, aspects related to activity, and correspondences. The objective of any spell you cast should be pure, and the spells in this chapter are only for protection. Each spell has some ingredients it needs for it to work. You can replace some of these depending on what works best for you. It is important to understand that not every ingredient needs to be used for you to cast a spell.

**Does Protection Magic Work Every Time?**

Protection spells may not work for you or your loved ones. This does not mean you should stop trying. You may have made a mistake when it came to your intent. The universe knows what you need and what you do not. Therefore, the universe will help you when you cast your spell. It is best to speak to the spirit and ask for its help to ensure the right things happen for you.

## Protection Sigils, Charms, and Stones

People often carry a stone they have carved their name in and use it as an amulet. They may also use a different object as an amulet, one they have energized. You can attribute different types of powers to any object so it acts as a talisman for you. The following are some examples of amulets:

1. You can use horsehair and blue beaded necklaces along with the evil eye.

2. Use either lapis lazuli, jade, or onyx if you want to improve your intelligence.

3. Wear amethysts, topazes, and red agates if you want to avoid headaches.

4. Use sapphires or rubies to overcome depression.

## Simple Protection Spells

Before you perform any spell, you need to perform an authentication ritual. When you perform this ritual before you cast any spell, you will focus on your objective. This ritual is also called the self-worship ritual, and you can either prepare your own or use the one mentioned in this section:

1. First, take a few deep breaths and count to ten.

2. Imagine a silver light is flowing through your body and into it. This energy is coming from the moon goddess.

3. As you continue breathing deeply, you can imagine a soft, golden light associated with the sun god flowing through your body.

4. Finally, visualize a white light moving into your body. This light is associated with the combined energy of universal love and universal life force.

Once you do this, say the following words aloud:

> *"Blessed be my feet walk the path of mystery.*
> *Blessed are my knees bending before the sacred altar.*
> *Blessed be my heart, molded-in beauty, and love.*
> *Blessed be my lips, who pronounce sacred names."*

Now you need to focus on love, happiness, and protection and open your arms wide. You can invite these emotions. Bring your arms back slowly towards your heart, indicating you have accepted these feelings from the universe. You can now end the ritual using the following words: "So be it. Now you can start casting."

Let us now look at some protection spells you can cast:

**Janus Protection Spell**

According to Greek mythology, Janus is the god of decisions and the god of all beginnings according to Roman mythology. When you cast this spell, you should request some help from the god. This is an easy spell for a beginner to cast. To perform this spell, you need the following:

- A slab of butter

- Half a cup of freshly brewed coffee

- A clean bowl

- A coffee filter

- Names of people you need protection from

Follow the steps given below to cast this spell:

1. Place the filter in the clean bowl. You need to draw a rune or magical symbol of Janus on the filter before you place it on the bowl

2. Now, add some butter to this filter and slowly heat it

3. Place the paper on the filter and leave it while the butter slowly melts

4. Pour the freshly brewed coffee over the filter, and ensure it covers the paper and butter

5. Now, ask God for help to protect you from these people

6. When you complete the spell, throw the mixture away. Ensure the mixture is nowhere close to you

This protection spell is the safest and easiest way to protect yourself from any enemies. You can also use it to fight any negative energy someone has cast on your life, goals, or you. It is best to repeat the spell every other week for a month to see results faster.

**Touch and Burn**

This is an interesting spell you can use to protect any of your belongings. It is a white magic spell so you can use it on any of your objects. You may want to protect some areas of your life, and you can use any object linked to this area to protect you. For example, if you want to protect your project or thesis, you can cast this spell on your project papers or documents. If you want to protect yourself financially, you can cast this spell on your purse or wallet. Alternatively, if you want to protect a loved one, you can cast this spell on any object belonging to him. You can also cast this spell on any object related to you and your loved one if you want to protect your relationship.

This spell is not very easy to cast and is very powerful. If you are casting this spell for the first time, you can try something easier first. To perform this spell, you need the following:

- A nail or pin

- White candle

- The object you want to cast a spell on

Follow the steps given below to perform the spell:

1.  Heat the tip of the nail or pin and write your name on the candle

2.  Place the candle on your altar and light it

3.  Once the flame turns mild, close your eyes. Focus on the intent and take a few deep breaths

4.  Now, visualize the candlelight removing the darkness in your mind. If you cannot do this, you can try to listen to the flame. You should keep doing this until you master the art

5.  After this, hold the object in both hands and say the following: "If you touch it, you will burn." Continue to say these words while you hold the object in your hands

6.  Visualize the light and heat from the candle penetrating this object. This would mean the object is extremely hot and nobody can touch it

7.  Once you do this, let the flame burn out

If you want to reinforce this spell, you should perform the above actions every Sunday during the day. Alternatively, you can choose to cast it on a full moon night. It is important to seal the object using your favorite symbol. You can protect everything using this spell. It is one of the safest spells to use to protect yourself from enemies.

## House Protection Spells

### Spell One

If you believe there is a lot of negative energy around you, you can use this spell. If you think someone is sending negative energy to your home, and you need to protect it, this is the spell for you. If you have not cast spells before, it is recommended you train and understand how spellcasting works. It is best for expert spellcasters to perform this spell.

In this spell, we will be calling out to a Celtic goddess, Brigid. It may seem strange to cast a spell with affirmations, prayers, and more. It is also difficult to commit yourself to this spell and focus on the words. Therefore, you should spend some time understanding how the spell works and get ready for it.

To perform this spell, follow the steps given below:

1. Choose the divine spirit that represents your beliefs. This spell uses Brigid, but you can choose to use another spirit you resonate with or connect with. Brigid is the goddess of fire and water, and she has healing powers which you can use to purify your house. It can help you remove any negative energy from your house. If you prefer not to invoke a divine spirit, you can refer to any other god you think can protect you.

2. Focus on the elements and visualize them flowing through your house. Visualize these elements removing any negative

energy from your house and pushing them through the windows and doors.

3.  When you are done with the visualization, stand in the center of your house and say the following:

*"I'm the wind on the sea.*

*They are ocean waves.*

*I am the roar of the sea.*

*I am a powerful ox.*

*I'm the hawk on the cliff.*

*I am a drop of dew in the sun.*

*I am the force of art.*

*I am a spear with loot engaged in battle*

*I cleaned the stony place on the mountain.*

*From the cellar to the attic, from the window to the door,*

*From the roof to the garden, I fill this house*

*Protective energy of (Name the chosen spirit)*

*And I ask the people here who reside*

*The blessings are dispensed.*

*So be it."*

You need to repeat this spell every two months to ensure your house is protected. Cast this spell either on a Sunday or Monday. Using this spell, you can affirm your house is your property. This spell can also be used if you want to protect yourself or a loved one. If you need to protect your loved one's home, go to their house, and cast this spell. Focus on the house and ask the spirit to protect it.

**Spell Two**

You can use this spell to protect your home using positive energy. This spell will help you create a powerful shield around your house, allowing you to remove any imbalances in the energy around your house. Using this spell, you can create a joyful, secure, and harmonious home environment for you and the people you love.

The potency of this spell, like every other spell, is dependent on your intent and focus. When your intent is clear, you can manifest it in the universe using the spell. If you cannot focus, wait until you feel better. Clear your mind and then try to cast this spell again.

This is a tricky spell, and it is important to ensure you abide by the rules and safety tips mentioned in the first chapter. You can also use a candle spell if you want to protect your home. The spell works much like the spell below and helps cast a warm glow and energize the protective forces around your house. This spell also makes it easier for you to remove any negative energy in your house.

To perform this spell, you need the following ingredients:

- A bowl (preferably one used for spell work)

- A handful of coarse salt

- 1 tsp minced garlic or garlic powder

Follow the steps given below to cast the spell:

1. Prepare the altar and place the bowl in the center. Now, add garlic and salt to it.

2. Mix the two ingredients and focus on your home. Imagine a layer of protection around your house since your home is a safe haven for you and your loved ones. Tell yourself that negative energy can't pass through the shield.

3. Once you visualize this, focus on how this shield will protect your house from any negative energy. You can feel the energy flowing from your body into the mixture of salt and garlic.

4. Now repeat the following words as you feel the energy flowing through your body:

*"With this salt, I cleanse this place*
*Let no one with ill intentions enter this space*
*Protect this space from all negative energies and entities*
*So, mote it be."*

5. Place a little bit of this mixture around your house. Move around your house in a clockwise direction and keep leaving the mixture in small quantities around the house

6. Visualize the protective energy from the mixture creating a shield around your house.

When it comes to sealing the house, you need to seal the windows and doorways to ensure no energy flows out of it. Once you do this, thank the Universe for protecting you and your home since you can live there. Let gratitude fill your body and wash away any negativity. Let the feeling of safety and warmth fill you.

**Enchanted Cord and Blessed Button Spell**

This protection spell works because of friendship and love alone. This spell can be used to protect yourself or a loved one. If you have someone you need to protect or has asked you to protect them, it indicates something negative is happening around them. In such cases, this is the best spell to cast.

When you cast this spell, you, or the person you want to protect, will feel a sense of safety and harmony. Be aware that it takes some time for this spell to manifest in the universe and protect you or your loved one. To perform this spell, you need:

- A string or ribbon of white cotton. You can also use a white chord.

- A button from your closest friends.

To perform this spell, follow the steps given below:

1. Use the string to connect the buttons you have collected. You can ask the divine spirit for love, luck, and protection. You can carry this with you everywhere you go to protect yourself and attract good luck. This can be used in all sorts of protective magic as well. If you believe you have a tough day ahead, you can leave this enchanted necklace close to your photo.

2. Once you have energized the chord with buttons, you can say the following words to make the chord an amulet:

*"As the cord is around the button*
*So, protection is around me (you)*
*Supported, secured, safe*
*A shield of protection is rising up."*

You can reinforce the spell every few weeks, especially on a Friday, to have the full effect. You can collect buttons for almost everybody you want to protect or heal and cast this spell.

## Handkerchief Enchantment

You can use this spell if you want to protect the people who live in the same house as you. If a family member needs to be protected, you should cast this spell. Do not use anything too fancy or hard when you perform this enchantment. The best thing for you to do is to cleanse your mind before you cast the spell. You may be wondering why you should do this.

You may have absorbed some of the fear, worry, or discomfort when you spoke to your family member. These feelings can seep into the spell when you cast it. Therefore, it is important to cleanse your mind of these feelings so you can begin casting the spell. You should be positive and open when you cast this spell. To perform this spell, you need the following:

- A white handkerchief representing every family member, along with their photograph

- Sea salt

- Springwater. You can also use tap water, but ensure you bless this on a new moon day before you use it for the spell

- Any protective incense

Follow the steps given below to cast the spell:

1. Open each handkerchief and spread it on the surface. Ensure they are not bent or folded anywhere

2. Sprinkle some sea salt and water on these handkerchiefs to purify them. Pick up the handkerchiefs and move them over the selected incense at least five times

3. Now, place the picture on top of the handkerchief associated with the person you want to protect. Next, cover the photo with your hands and say the following words:

> *"And the Spirit did miracles by the hands*
> *of the children of God,*
> *So, they could bring aid to the sick and fearful,*
> *To heal diseases and free them from evil spirits."*

4. Now, visualize and focus on the pure white light. This light is entering your body from the top of your body and making its way slowly to the bottom. It should enter your body through the crown chakra and slowly move into all the organs in your body

5. If you find yourself losing focus and concentration, breathe deeply for a while to regain your focus. You need to breathe

and seal this spell if you think you are done with casting it. Once you end the spell, fold your palms in the shape of a cross over the handkerchief and photo

6. Repeat the process with all the other pictures

Once you are done, you should thank the spirit you chose or visualized for guiding you. Give the person you have protected the handkerchief and ask them to carry it with them. This handkerchief is now their amulet.

## Points to Remember

You need to think about the following rules when you perform any protection spell or any other white magic.

- It is important to focus on the alternatives before you cast a protective spell for yourself or a loved one. If you have trouble with certain people, see if you can address the issue by speaking to them. If you have tried every non-magic method and nothing seems to work for you, you can use the spells in this chapter or those we will look at in the subsequent chapter

- If someone is abusing or harassing you, speak to someone about it quickly. Speak to a loved one or friend and ask them for their opinion

- Do not try and harm someone through magic since there are consequences. Anything you put out in the universe can deflect back to you and affect you

- Never wait for too long before you react to something. You need to have the courage and nerves to perform the protection spell. Do not let negative energy surround you and envelope you because it will only get stronger. If the energy is strong, it will be hard for you to overcome it

- If you perform any spell ethically, legally, or morally wrong, you cannot expect the magic to protect you. If there is something you need help with, ask the universe for guidance. Focus on what the universe says and fix the issue. If you are trying to rectify a mistake you have made, the universe may choose to fix the issue the way it believes it should and not worry about you

- If you want to protect a loved one, first ask them if you can cast a spell on them. Alternatively, if you choose to do it without letting them know, then you should remove any negative feelings and thoughts. Your intention to cast the spell should come from your heart.

# Chapter Nine

## Protecting Yourself
## from Challenging People

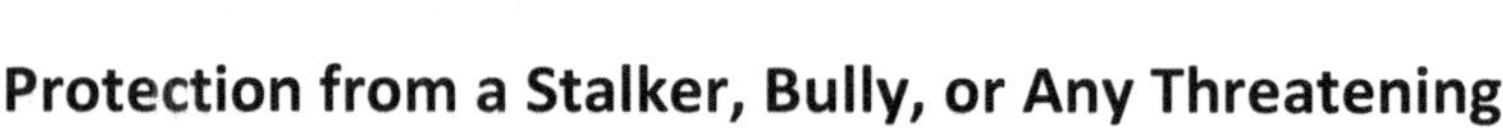

**Protection from a Stalker, Bully, or Any Threatening Individual**

Before you perform this spell, ensure you have done everything you can to protect yourself from the person threatening or harassing you in the physical world. Speak to the police, increase security measures around your house, change your locks, and block this person from all social media, your phone, and more.

If this person has given you something, and you still have it at home, take it out. This can be something as simple as a note or a painting in your house. Do not use this object if you need to use it as evidence for later. Move this object away from your person before you cast the spell at home.

The objective of this spell is to free your home of any negative energy emanating from your harasser. Alternatively, you can try to separate yourself from this so no energy connects you to the person. The same can be said for your social world as well – you need to remove the person's presence from your text history, email, voicemails, etc. Put any information you can use to protect yourself in a folder in case you need to provide it as evidence. If you do not need it, you can delete it.

Once you do this, you are ready to cast the protection spell. Experts recommend you cast this spell on a Sunday, Tuesday, or Saturday. It is on these days the moon is present on the fire signs, Sagittarius, Aries, and Leo. If you need to perform this spell as an emergency, you can do it whenever you need to.

To perform this spell, you need the following items:

- 2 drops of frankincense essential oil

- Sunflower oil

- A small glass bottle

Before you cast the spell, you need to call the Archangel Michael. To do this, say the following sentence aloud: "Archangel Michael, I call on you."

Now, uncork the glass bottle and pour the sunflower oil until you fill half the bottle. Pour the frankincense essential oil into the bottle and put the cork in. Now shake the oils gently to combine them. You can say the following words while holding this bottle in your hands:

*"Thank you for filling this oil*
*with your fiery, protective light."*

Now, focus on the bottle and visualize yourself being covered by the brightness of the Archangel. Uncork the bottle and dip the tip of your index finger in the blended oil. Place a little oil on your heart, belly, and forehead. If you do not want to put the oil on your skin, you can inhale the fragrance. Visualize yourself being enveloped in the brightness of the Archangel. Now, cast the spell:

*"Thank you for surrounding me with*
*a fiery wall of light and protecting me from all harm,*
*physical, emotional, and spiritual."*

Visualize yourself being covered in the light and thank the Archangel for being present when you cast the spell.

Now close the circle and use the blended oil to anoint your house. Dab a little oil on all the doors and windows. This will signal the energy outside to flow into your house. Move in a clockwise direction while you anoint. If you want to be very careful, you can anoint everything you use or touch. Ensure you protect yourself from all harm. You can carry this oil in your bag and refresh the protection spell whenever you need to.

## Protection from Dysfunctional or Overbearing Relatives

Everybody has relatives whose actions and words affect them. This may be the case for you too. Before you choose to use a protection spell, ask yourself the following questions:

- Did you speak to your relatives and tell them how you feel when they pass comments or judgment?

- Have you learned to set boundaries with the person so they do not say or do anything to hurt you?

- Do you need to confront them and have an uncomfortable conversation about protecting yourself from these situations?

When it comes to relatives, you can assume how they will react to what you must say to them. For instance, you may have already told yourself how the relative may respond to you if you do choose to speak up about how their treatment affects you. You think you cannot confront them or speak up because if you do, they will say or do something.

You are probably right, but you never know. People do surprise you. Having said that, it is best to initiate this conversation to ensure you are doing whatever you can before you resort to magic. If you have handled the situation in the best way possible by speaking to them, you can choose to use a spell to protect yourself.

You can also use protective spells to set boundaries. Alternatively, you can set boundaries by telling them you are not willing to speak to them anymore until you feel seen, respected, or listened to. If you are being pressured to spend time with this relative by a loved one, you can speak to them first about why you no longer want to communicate with the person. You can tell them how you feel, and honor this truth. In any case, listen to your inner voice and do what feels right to you. This is not fun to do, but you can call your power back and see how you feel about it. Ensure you keep your eye on the prize.

If you believe you need to use magic to protect yourself, use your energy to protect yourself from this relative despite the considerations you have taken. This spell is for you if you no longer have the tolerance to deal with this relative.

This is a very simple spell, and you need to begin with calling on a divine helper or the Divine in any way you believe is right. You need to use a black tourmaline when you perform this spell. This crystal will absorb any negative energy coming your way when you perform the spell. You can also use this crystal to protect yourself from family members in the future. Carry this crystal with you everywhere you go.

If you believe a relative is affecting you from afar or draining your energy, you should wear this crystal at all times and not only when you are around the relative. Experts recommend you sleep with this crystal on your person too. Due to the spell, the dynamic will improve, and you will heal. Afterward, you may not need the crystal any longer. However, you still need to learn to protect yourself from any mental or physical challenges the relative may put you through.

## Protection from a Gaslighter

The term gaslighting was popularized when the movie Gaslight was released in 1944. The term means to mislead someone without giving any thought to their feelings or emotions. It also means to convince someone they are wrong or crazy. You can also think about how Emily Blunt in 'Girl on the Train' was made to think she was crazy. This is an example of gaslighting.

You can gaslight someone in different ways. Simple questions can be loaded with a lot of subtexts, and they can indicate disrespect. When they ask you why you are angry, they may indicate something wrong with you for feeling this way. They may also be under the assumption that normal people would never let something this trivial affect them.

It also does not hurt to check yourself and see if something you have done has made them believe you are wrong to feel the way you feel. For instance, if someone were to ask you why you are angry, you can pause and think about why you feel the way you do. You will know exactly why you are angry and can list the reasons if asked. You may also discover that you are angry because of something from the past and not what is happening to you now. In some cases, the person asking you why you feel the way you do may not even have understood why you felt this way. He may have asked you the question to understand you better.

All I am trying to say is uncomfortable conversations do not necessarily indicate gaslighting. It is often difficult to differentiate between gaslighting and regular conversation, especially if you are talking to someone you have a good relationship with.

If you are unsure of being gas lit, speak to a family member or friend. You can explain the situation to them and understand their perspective as well. This will bring a lot of clarity to the situation and change your perception. You can then determine if you do need to perform the protection spell. Using this spell, you can recognize gaslighting and protect yourself from it too.

To perform this spell, you need the following:

- A mister containing rose water

- Use a polished Howlite crystal. If you have any jewelry with this crystal, you can use it, too. Energize this crystal in the sun for a few minutes

- 4 drops of geranium essential oil

It is best to perform this spell on a day when the moon is between new and full. This usually happens on a Sunday. You should first cast the protection circle and hold the crystal in your dominant hand. Once you do this, say the following words: "Archangel Raphael, bring me clarity. Archangel Michael, bring me strength."

Move the crystal into your pocket or wear the jewelry with this crystal. Now, pour the essential oil in the mister of rose water. Close this mister and blend the liquids gently. Hold this mister in your non-dominant hand and say the following words: "Archangel Raphael, fill me with clarity. Archangel Michael, fill me with strength."

Spray this blended liquid around you thrice. If you have sensitive skin, be careful about how you use essential oils. If you do not believe it is good to use an essential oil on your skin, smell the fragrance. While you do this, visualize yourself being enveloped in bright light.

If you are sure you are going to meet the gaslighter on a certain day, wear this crystal on your person and carry the mist with you.

Alternatively, you can inhale the blended potion. When you do this, visualize yourself within a sphere of clear, white light.

## Protection from a Critic

Do you know a person who is constantly criticizing everything you say or do? Is this person bringing your spirits down? If this is the case, you should first ask yourself what makes you feel this way. You should also check if you want to end the relationship and how you can do it. If you think you can do it, you do not need to use a spell. Just leave and never look back.

If you do not think it is this easy, first check if you have talked to the person about this. See if you have discussed with him why you want to end the relationship or what affects you. Did you ask the person to stop being the way he is with you? Did you tell them how you feel when they treat you a certain way? If you have not done this, it is recommended that you do this. You can also speak to a friend or family member about this issue to help you assess and understand your thoughts.

Do not deal with the situation in a passive-aggressive way. Protection spells do not mean you should stop being assertive. Conversations can be uncomfortable, but you should have this conversation with them to ensure you feel better. If you do not think you can have this conversation, speak to a therapist or psychiatrist if you need to understand the situation better. It is best to begin here instead of using magic to solve the problem.

If you have looked at all options and yet find yourself being forced to spend time with the person, you can protect yourself by using the following spell. To perform the spell, you only need aura quartz. You can choose any color you connect with.

Before you cast this spell, you should cast a protective circle around you. Hold the crystal in your hands and call on the Divine spirit. You can call on the spirit in any way that feels natural. Say your spell out loud and say these words with intent. This is the only way you can protect yourself. You should cast this spell pretending you are speaking to someone you love most. Talk about how you feel and how the spell can help you. You can either carry this crystal or wear it if you need to.

## Protection at Work

Using this protective spell, you can protect yourself from any negativity at your workplace. It is best to cast this spell either a day after or before the full moon. Before you perform this spell, you need to gather the following:

- Use a charm depicting an eye, hamsa, or mirrored tile. This charm can be embedded in a pendant. You can also use a long chain if you want to and wear it if you do not want this pendant and charm to be seen.

- White candle and white cloth

Before you cast your protective circle, you should go outside, light the candle, and spread the cloth. If you are casting the spell when there is light, you can avoid using the candle. You only need to spread the cloth so it can absorb the energy from the sun. Now, place the pendant on the cloth and let it absorb the energy. If there is no sunlight, use the candle to energize the charm.

Once you cast the circle, hold this charm in your hands and call on the spirit. After you do this, repeat the following thrice: "Thank you for protecting me at work. Thank you for protecting my mind, body, spirit, and aura. Thank you for helping me to stay energized and positive, and thank you for deflecting any and all negativity straight back to its source. Thank you, thank you, thank you. Blessed be. And so, it is."

## Protection from Mental and Physical Harm

This protection spell is one you can use to save yourself from being physically or mentally harmed by someone. It is different from the one we looked at above. Using this spell, you can shield yourself from toxic people or when someone causes you mental harm by never letting you go. This spell can also be used to protect yourself from any unpleasantness, and must be repeated numerous times to ensure it retains its power.

An advantage of using this spell is that it is based on white magic and will not harm anybody. When you cast this spell, you do not manipulate another individual. Use the energy from within you and the Earth when you cast the spell. When you collect enough energy, you can make the spell more powerful.

The spell will also last longer. Visualize the person in a shiny layer of energy, like a protective bubble around them. The negative energy emanating from the person stays within this bubble. This layer will not let any of their energy, positive or negative, exit. So, if they think of any loving thoughts, it helps them, and they benefit from it. If they think cruel thoughts about others, they will be the ones to suffer and nobody else.

Light a candle and visualize the person in front of you. If you are unable to visualize them, use their picture. Place the picture in front of the candle and assume there is a layer around them. Repeat the following words thrice:

*"All acts of negativity will now return to thee.*
*All bad you try to send my way upon your own self will hold sway.*
*All actions, thoughts, and words of hate become*
*your own decided fate.*
*By all up high, the world and wise*
*By oceans wide and deep blue skies*
*By day and night, and powers three*
*This is my will, so it must be.*
*Harm to none, nor return on me."*

# Chapter Ten

# Feng Shui

Feng Shui is based on the concept of the Bagua and finding a way to harmonize the five elements. It is easy to strike a balance between these energies using the Bagua. The Bagua is a chart used by people all over the world to understand the power of energy in different parts of the house and the area surrounding the house.

The chart is shaped like a turtle's shell, and it provides a layout with nine different locations synonymous with different areas of your life. These interlinked sectors also depict how the energy in these areas of your life affects you.

The energies around you affect the way you think and feel. Therefore, it is important to strike a balance between these energies. This is the only way you can be at peace, and when you find this level of unity, you can prosper. This chapter deals with the eight factors and will help you understand them much better.

## Fire

The fire sector in the Bagua chart is the most important sector since it deals with enlightenment and learning. If you balance the energy in this sector, it becomes easier for you to learn more about different aspects of your life. The energy in this sector also helps you determine if you need something in your life. Using the energy in this sector, you can identify your dreams and do everything in your power to achieve your goals. This indicates that you can also achieve the desired results of any spell you cast.

Once you balance the energy in this sector, you can ask yourself the right questions and determine the approach you want to take to achieve the goal. You can determine if you want to cast the spell or need someone to help you keep your goal in mind. Spellcasting takes a lot of effort, so it is important to determine if you have the right thoughts in mind before you cast the spell.

## Water

The energy in this sector soothes you. It has a very strong effect on every aspect of your life and also helps you determine if you have chosen the right career path. The energy in this sector affects the way you perceive work and your colleagues. If you want to cast a spell to improve your working conditions or change your relationship with your colleagues, balance the energy in this sector. You may also have a lot of questions about your life, and you can use the energy in this sector to help you answer those questions.

**Earth**

The energy in the Earth sector keeps you grounded. It will also keep you confident about the relationship you are in. Using the energy in this sector, you can determine if you have the right idea about the people you want to start a new relationship with. It is important to sit down in this sector and balance the energies in your mind and the sector before you cast a binding spell. The energy in this sector not only talks about romantic or familial relationships but also about your social relationships.

Using the energy in this sector, you can determine if you are happy about your relationship. It is important to fill this sector with positive energy to ensure you remain happy and peaceful. Using this energy, it becomes easier for you to understand the depth of the relationship.

**Mountain**

The energy in the mountain sector enables you to determine how you deal with different situations. It also helps you understand and accept the existence of a higher power. The energy in this sector can give you confidence and improve your self-esteem. Ancient Chinese texts associate the mountain sector in the Bagua chart to a person's self-esteem and self-confidence.

The energy flowing through this sector makes it easier for you to tread the right path towards your spirituality. It becomes easier for you to calm your mind and meditate in this sector in your house. It is best to sit in this sector before you cast a spell to focus your thoughts.

**The Lake**

The energy in this sector emphasizes your creativity. The energy makes it easier for you to understand your capacity. If the energy in this sector is well balanced, it indicates that your relationship with your offspring will improve. Ensure this part of your house is set up the right way. If there are objects that hinder the flow of energy in this sector, it is going to be harder for you to manage and maintain your relationship with your family.

The energy in this sector is also an indicator of your creativity. It becomes easier for you to understand your creativity and assess if you are using it the right way. It will also become easier for you to be creative when you cast a spell. It does help if you use theatrics when you cast spells, and the energy in this sector will make it easier for you to do this.

**Thunder**

The thunder sector in the Bagua chart is important to consider when it comes to balancing the energy in your house. You need to carefully assess the energy in this sector to ensure your house is filled with positive energy. The energy in this sector will help you understand and assess the relationship you share with:

- The people and community you live in

- The elders in your family.

Using the energy in this sector, you can answer a few of the questions mentioned below:

1.  Were there times when you had felt family members underappreciated you?

2.  Have you had a good relationship with your mentors and your teachers?

3.  Have you had loving memories with your family and your parents?

## Heaven

Heaven, as the name suggests, focuses on your spirituality. It focuses on how you view God. You can understand your level of compassion for different aspects of your life. If the energy in this sector is balanced, you can identify the people around you who genuinely love and those who only choose to cause harm. The energy in this sector also gives you the sense your loved ones will protect you from any harm and be there in your times of need.

## The Wind

The wind has a lot of energy, and it is important to learn to change the way the energy flows. This is the only way to change various aspects of your life. The wind carries blessings from people, and if you use this energy wisely, you can prosper and succeed in any venture. It becomes easier for you to understand your financial status. The energy in the wind also makes it easier for you to gain more wealth and fame through the path you have chosen. Balancing the energy in this sector is key if you want to free yourself of worry.

**The Tai Chi**

The Tai Chi sector in the Bagua chart focuses on Chi. Chi is the force of energy found everywhere in the universe. It is your life force. When you cast a spell using an object, you can use this energy to fill the object since chi can permeate any animate or inanimate object.

## Methods to Strike a Balance Between These Energies

In the previous sections, we looked at the different sectors in the Bagua chart you can use to balance the energies in your house. We also looked at the importance of trying to strike this balance. The objective is to ensure you feel at peace. It is important to learn how to balance the energies in your home if you choose to cast spells at home. Any negative energy in your house can make it harder for you to cast the spell. Ensure you strike a balance between the following pairs of sectors to have a flow of positive energy throughout your home.

1.  Earth and Heaven

2.  Mountain and Lake

3.  Water and Fire

4.  Thunder and Wind

You may now wonder why it is important for you to strike a balance between the energies in these sectors. Let us go through the different pairs to give you a better idea.

## Water and Fire

Using the energy in the fire sector, you can work towards enlightenment and illumination. How enlightened do you want to be, though? Do you want to learn about something and then stop because you believe you have learned everything there is to learn about the subject? It is important to learn constantly to ensure your knowledge does not stagnate. The energy from the water sector balances the energy in the fire sector, thereby ensuring you are content and happy.

## Mountain and Lake

When you have the lake sector around you, you will find your creativity has enhanced, and you work well on anything you pursue. Let us assume you have decided to build a new house. You let your creativity loose and choose to have different colored sections in your house. You may choose to paint the walls in the living room in different colors. This is only going to make your house look strange. You need to channel your creativity the right way, and this is where the energy from the mountain sector will come to your aid.

## Wind and Thunder

Wind and thunder are intertwined and closely connected. The wind is associated with blessings, while thunder is associated with any relationship you share with your elders. It is important to balance these energies so you can restore the balance in your relationships.

## Earth and Heaven

This last pair is extremely important since you must know if you share a great relationship with your friends. The dynamics of the relationship become clear when you learn how to balance the energy in this sector.

Understand the different sectors and how these relate to each other. When you understand this, you can balance the energies in the sector and the flow of this energy. It is also important to understand this balance if you want to ensure universal energy flows freely through the sector. Ensure you have good relationships with your friends and your family. You must also ensure you strike a balance between your creativity and your mountain to ensure you never do something extravagant. You will find yourself at peace when you strike a balance between the different energies.

If you are going to cast spells at home, it is best to use the techniques mentioned in this chapter to neutralize the energy in the house.

# Chapter Eleven

## Spells to Protect Your Happiness and Energy

If you need to perform a spell to uplift your energy and spirits, you can use the spells in this chapter. These spells give you access to the unlimited power reserve of the Earth to restore your energy.

### Energy Protection Spell

As the name suggests, this spell is used to reignite or replenish a diminishing spirit. It is easy to perform and gives you just enough firepower to make sure you are back in the driver's seat.

To cast this spell, you will need:

- One orange candle

- A cinnamon stick

- Orange yarn

- A heatproof dish

Ensure the yarn is at least long enough to be spun around the candle a few times. Follow the steps below to perform the spell:

1.  Prepare yourself before you cast the spell

2.  Take the candle and wrap the yarn around it. While you wrap the yarn, tie knots. Ensure the knots are equidistant from each other on the surface of the candle.

3.  After you do this, set the candle in a holder and leave it on the altar.

4.  Now, prepare yourself and focus on the spell.

5.  Block out all distractions, dive deep into your mind, and look for the energy you need. If you did this correctly, you would feel the energy surging up from your feet into your head. With the body and mind filled with energy, ignite the candle, and begin the following chant: "Energy, power, rise up the tower." Repeat these words aloud at least four times.

6.  Now hold one end of the cinnamon stick and move the other towards the candle.

7.  Once the candle lights up, let it burn and sustain its flame for a few moments. Once the candle's flame becomes consistent, set it down gently in the heatproof dish. As the flame eats the candle away, make sure you focus on the fire's energy as it consumes the candle.

If you want this spell to work for you, your concentration on the flame should not be disturbed. Do not lose focus until the candle depletes itself entirely.

## Spell to Attract Positive Energy

This spell will bring you a breath of positive air when you need it the most. To perform this spell, you need:

- Three yellow or orange candles

- 4 drops of cedar oil

- A pinch of marjoram or rosemary

Follow the steps below to perform the spell:

1. Apply oil on all three candles and place them on the altar

2. Light the candles in order and sprinkle some of the herbs on them

3. Focus and prepare yourself and turn your attention to the flames

4. Join your palms and move them over the flames. Once you can feel the radiant energy of the fire, channel its power, and repeat the following aloud:

> *"Happiness and joy come into my life.*
> *Away with anger, stress, and strife*
> *I am happy; I am free*
> *No more negativity."*

## Protection from Unhappiness

**Winds of Joy**

This spell can be used to protect yourself and your loved ones from unhappiness. This spell is called Winds of Joy and is designed to help you get rid of feelings of doubt, anxiety, and other emotions preventing you from experiencing happiness. This spell not only requires ingredients but also requires ideal weather conditions as well. It is best to perform this spell on a windy day. Apart from this, you only need patchouli and basil.

To perform the spell, follow the steps below:

1. Choose the spot where you want to cast the spell

2. Carry the herbs to the chosen spot and stand with your back facing the wind

3. Toss the herbs into the air and visualize your problems floating away like the herbs carried by the wind

4. Stand at the spot, take deep breaths, and focus on the wind for some time

5. Visualize your problems separating from you and let their place be taken by peace and quiet.

6. Once you do this, repeat the following words at least three times:

> *"May the winds take my pain.*
> *Make me happy once again.*

7.  Now, face the wind and say the following:

*"May the winds bring joy to me.*
*So happy I will be"*

**Flowers of Happiness**

This spell uses the energy from fresh flowers to create positive vibes to help you deal with any unhappiness. To make this potion, you need:

- Jasmine or lilac essential oil

- Any fresh flower (you can choose the one you prefer)

- A yellow candle

- A heatproof container

- Paper and pencil

Follow the steps given below to perform the spell:

1.  List the three situations where you feel unhappy. Once you identify these, write them down on paper.

2.  Now, light the candle and focus on the flame. Take the piece of paper and set it ablaze using the candle's flame and allow it to burn itself to nothingness. When the paper is almost burnt, leave it in the bowl and let the flame consume it.

3. Apply the essential oil on the flower and inhale the smell. Now visualize the problems fading away and disappearing as the paper did.

4. To complete the spell, you must be able to visualize the beautiful flower taking the place of your problems. When you have this image in your mind, place the flower on top of the ash in the bowl.

5. Finally, leave the bowl and the flower on the altar to remind you to find happiness in any situation in life.

# Chapter Twelve

## Binding Spells to Protect
## a Loved One from Harm

A binding spell can be used to help people and protect them from curses or hexes. You can use binding spells to protect someone you love. There are two types of binding spells:

1.  Binding two people using a love spell

2.  Restricting someone's actions

You should use every binding spell with caution. Ensure you give this spell a lot of thought before you cast it.

### Why Should You Avoid Binding Lovers Together?

It is never a good idea to bind people together using a binding spell since it can cause a lot of complications and misery later. One exception is where the couple chooses to bind themselves together but follow the ritual to the tee. The ritual they perform is only for a specific period, and they can choose to re-cast the spell every year if they want to do so.

Think about the following example: You love someone dearly and think she is the love of your life. You believe she is the one for you, and you decide the two of you should stay together. So, you choose to use a binding spell to ensure nobody comes between you and her. After you cast the binding spell, you are happy for a few years, but then you realize the two of you are not suited for each other. Since you cast the binding spell, the two of you cannot get away from each other no matter how hard you try. You would need to remove the spell using different detangling spells, but this would be difficult for you to do.

There have been cases where a binding spell has changed people's personalities. So, avoid using binding spells unless you know what you are doing. It is risky to use binding spells on lovers because it can be difficult to break the spell if needed. Do not use the spells in this chapter on your lover since it is too risky.

## Binding a Controller, Bully, or Tormentor

There are many people out there who may want to target you or overpower you. They may do this by frightening you or even controlling you. This will make you feel terrified, frustrated, and powerless. It could be someone at work, school, your partner, or even a guardian. In such situations, you should use a binding spell to help you overcome any troubles you are facing. Let us look at some situations where you can use a binding spell:

- A colleague constantly picks faults and meddles in all your work, and this makes work miserable.

- A bully is tormenting your child or loved one

- An ex-girlfriend or boyfriend who cannot move on from you and is harassing and forcing you to get back together with them

- A partner who is tracking your every move and trying to control you. In such cases, a binding spell can prevent them from affecting you and help you come out of the relationship

- A neighbor or stalker who constantly spies on you

- Someone who is doing their best to run you out of business

- Using a spell on your loved ones to protect them from someone who is trying to cause any harm

**When Should You Not Use a Binding Spell?**

- You should avoid using a binding spell in the following situations:

- You want to take revenge on someone for hurting you or a loved one

- You are upset with how people are treating you

- The person has a mental health issue

- You find someone behaving differently than they usually do

- If you are young and overreacting

- If you want to do something illegal

**Can You Use Something Instead of a Binding Spell?**

You do not have to cast a binding spell on someone. You can choose to perform a less powerful action or spell. You can choose from numerous magical techniques, but these may not be as powerful. Using these techniques, you can move the magical power into your hands and avoid sending anything negative to the people you want to cast a spell on but don't forget that a binding spell also has grave consequences. The following are alternatives to performing a binding spell on any individual.

- Instead of casting a binding spell, you can speak to the person and ask them to look at things positively

- Use a protective charm or crystal

- If there is a spell cast on another person, you can choose to reverse it or neutralize it. Do not choose a binding spell if you know you can do this.

- Look at things differently. When someone yells at you, they can seem frightening. If you focus on their antics and activities, you will see the funny side of things. This will remove any negativity you feel towards the person

- Use a protection spell instead of a binding spell

- Use Feng Shui to remove any negative energy from your home. We will look at some techniques in the next chapter you can use to change the flow of energy in your house

- If you do not think this is practical, use visualization techniques to surround yourself with positivity

**Do You Still Need To Use a Binding Spell?**

You now know what a binding spell is and its effects on people. If you still believe you need to cast a binding spell, you need to be prepared.

## Precautions

It is best to wait a few days or weeks before you cast a binding spell on another person. Experts recommend you explore all other options first before you choose a binding spell. For example, if your child or loved one is being bullied in school or university, you can first speak to the teachers. Before you do this, see if the situation can be sorted between the bully and your loved one. Do not jump to the conclusion of using a binding spell only because you know you can since this can make the situation worse.

Perform a risk assessment and look at the consequences of a binding spell. Understand how the spell can affect the universe and the type of energy you are putting out there. If you know how to read tarot cards, it is best to perform a reading to understand the outcome of any spell you cast. Alternatively, you can use a mind map to help you assess why you want to perform the spell. Use this map also to map out any consequence of the binding spell on yourself and the person you are casting this spell on. You should also see if it could harm anybody else in case you have someone else in mind when you cast the spell. It is difficult to cover all your bases, but it is important to try and do this.

Ensure you want to perform the spell for the right reasons. Your intentions and thoughts must be pure. Do not cause mental or physical harm to anybody. Your spell should only focus on controlling a person's vindictive behavior towards you. Never perform a binding spell if you know the person you are casting it on knows how magic works. If the person notices you are casting a binding spell on them, they will most definitely send the spell back your way. In such situations, it is best to find another way to approach the problem.

**Why Should You Not Perform the Spell in Anger?**

Any spell you cast is dependent on your emotions, thoughts, and intentions. Therefore, you need to cast a spell only if you feel at peace. Do not cast the spell if you are guilty, angry, depressed, afraid, or stressed. If you have negative emotions when you cast the spell, you will risk increasing the magnitude of these feelings. If you recollect the information from before, you know magic relies on the principle of the law of attraction, i.e., like attracts like. Therefore, if you have negative emotions when you cast a spell, you will be pushing those emotions into the universe. The universe will then put you in similar situations because of how you feel. Therefore, you need to focus on your feelings and thoughts when you cast spells and ensure they are positive and pure.

**What Do You Need to Cast a Binding Spell?**

The following items are what you need to perform a binding spell:

- Any object representing the person you want to cast a spell on. This object can be a sturdy twig, doll, wooden spoon, clothespin, cardboard piece, paper, etc. It is best if you can write the name of the person on the object.

- Strong thread or ribbon between 12 and 24 inches in length. The length is dependent on the object being used to perform the spell.

**Working on the Ritual**

You don't need to cast a protective circle when you perform a binding spell, but you can if you want to. If you are using a poppet for the binding spell, you can write the name of the person anywhere you can. If you cannot write it anywhere on the poppet or the object you are using, you can simply name the object with the person's name.

Sit down for a few minutes before you cast the spell. Understand how you feel and focus on your thoughts and emotions. Since your thoughts and emotions are what give your magic power, it is best to keep them pure. You can focus on how the person affects you. Focus on the fear or pain the person causes you, but only for a few seconds. Now, imagine how you would feel if the feelings stopped and focus on the relief. Focus on this relief and feel the sense of happiness flowing through your body. Focus on your emotions and hold them in your mind when you cast the spell.

Hold the poppet or any other object with your non-dominant hand and the ribbon or cord in your dominant one. Now, place the string or cord against the object, hold it in place using your non-dominant hand's thumb, and slowly wind the string around it. Now, say the following words:

**Their name* you gotta stop*
*Your cruel behavior, I've had enough*
*No longer will you cause me trouble*
*Or Karma upon you will be treble*
*As I bind you, I am free*
*You never bother me more.*

You can change the spell to whatever works best for you, depending on your situation. Repeat these words thrice and feel the emotions of peace and happiness flowing through you. Now, complete the spell by saying the following:

*As I intend, so must it be.*

It is possible you may get a few words wrong, but this does not matter. Spell casting is only about your intentions, thoughts, feelings, and energy. When you are done with the spell, tuck the end of the string or cord and relax. The spell is now done. Keep the object safe since you may want to remove the string from around the object and unbind the person.

## Five Ways to Use Binding Spells to Protect Loved Ones

### Binding Spell for Protection

Your love for a friend, family member, partner, or anybody else, will push you to protect them. If you know someone is trying to harm them, you will do everything in your power to keep them safe. If you want to use a binding spell on your loved one, choose a picture of your loved one where he is happy and joyous. Experts recommend you use a picture that's in a silver frame since silver is associated with good spirits.

You also need to have:

- An altar

- A candle

- Basil

Now cleanse yourself completely and meditate before you sit down to cast the spell. Remove any negative thoughts you may have and focus on the person. Light the candle and look at the flame. Chant the verse you have prepared for your loved one slowly. Do not let any negative thoughts enter your mind when you cast the spell since this can have negative effects on the person.

**Hand Fasting Spell**

These types of spells are often cast in Western Europe. You do not use an object here but hold hands with your loved one. When you cast this spell, you need to tie a ribbon around your hands. This ribbon is associated with a symbol of love and commitment between you and your loved one. The spell is often used to join two people in matrimony. In the Eragon book series, Eragon binds Roran and Katrina together using a ribbon. This ribbon is a symbol of togetherness.

## Casting the Enemy Away

Not everybody is good, and some people are extremely evil. These people do not like anything good happening to the people around them. You may have come across such people at one point in life. You may also have enemies who are jealous of your successes in life. You can cast a spell in such situations to ensure your enemy does not affect you at any point in life. Most people believe they can only use black magic in such cases, but you can use the binding spell mentioned below to do this.

To perform this spell, you need:

- An altar

- A purple candle with a purple wick

- A picture of your enemy

- The altar circle where you will place the purple candle

- A stapler

You first need to fold the picture of your enemy in half and seal the picture using a stapler. When you do this, you should chant the spell you have written, casting the enemy away. Once this is done, use the stapler to join the photograph in the middle of the calendar. This will help you seal the spell.

## Binding an Amulet Using a Protection Spell

An amulet can attract happiness and good things into the life of those who wear it. So, it is best to give your loved one an amulet, isn't it? Since you do want to protect your loved one from harm, you can give them an amulet if you cannot repeatedly use spells to protect your loved one. You can also use white magic to protect your loved one. So, cast a protection spell on the amulet and ask your loved one to wear it regularly. This amulet will add some protection to the wearer. This amulet can be anything including a pendant, necklace, bracelet, or something similar. Choose an amulet the person will wear.

# Chapter Thirteen

# How to Remove Black Magic?

**B**lack magic is a dark form of magic, which we have looked at earlier in the book. This chapter will look at how you can protect yourself from black magic or remove it.

## Know If You Are Cursed

### Ask Yourself If Someone Has a Reason

Do you believe someone would want to curse you? Think about why you believe you are cursed. Do you know someone out there who wants you to fail? You cannot expect to be cursed by someone who does not know you. It is not common for one to be cursed by black magic. Therefore, if you are cursed, it is because the people around you have a problem with you. The following are some types of hexes or curses a person could have cast on you:

- Revenge spell

- Anger curse

- Series of bad dreams spell

- Insomnia spell

- Love hex

The last type of spell is only a problem if you have been forced to fall in love if you did not want to.

**See If You Have Had a Series of Bad Luck**

If Lady Luck has not been on your side for the last few weeks or months, it indicates someone has cast a spell on you. If one issue after the other occurs or there is something off in your life, it is possible you need to remove the negative spell and energy cast on you. The following are a few examples of when such situations could have occurred:

- You have been falling ill quite often, and it is not the common cold

- You are doing badly at work or on a test, although you have done your best to do well

- You have a bad acne breakout before you go out

- You fall often and you do not know why this happens because you are careful

- Your car breaks down often and this makes it hard for you to reach your appointments on time

**Understand Everything Bad Happening around You is Not a Curse**

It is important to understand that your luck does not have to do with being cursed by someone around you. You may have some enemies, but someone can't have the power to curse you if they are far away. Think about what is happening to you and see if things could be happening because of something else. If you do not think there is any other reason, and you are sure someone out there has cursed you, use the techniques mentioned below to rid yourself of the magic.

- For instance, if your siblings suddenly begin fighting with you or distancing themselves from you, it could be because someone cast a spell on you. Alternatively, they could be doing it because of some underlying issues

- If you have issues with your health, it could be because of the change in the weather and not because someone has it in for you

If you are certain someone is out there wishing you harm, take the necessary steps to reverse this spell.

## Cleansing Your Spirit

**Use Amulets**

You can protect yourself and your loved ones using an amulet. This is an object you need to carry with you. This object can protect you from hexes, curses, and bad energy. If you keep this amulet with you, it can weaken the effects of any hex or curse, and this will not harm you anymore.

Amulets can be anything. They can be any object that means something to you and is sacred to you. You can use a pebble from the park you frequently visit, the ribbon or clothes you wore as a child or even special jewelry. You need to wear this object regularly. Alternatively, you can carry this on your person.

**Bathe in Magic Herbs and Salt**

If you choose to bathe in magic herbs and salt, understand that they cleanse harmful energy. If you think you have been cursed, you can draw a warm bath and light candles around the bath. Focus only on positive thoughts as you soak for a long time. Use one of the following in your bath to increase the power of the bath:

- Hyssop

- Mugwort

- Salt

- Basil

- Wormwood

- Vetiver

- Patchouli

**Burn Incense**

You can use the same magic herbs to remove any negative energy focused on you. These herbs can be used to break any hex or curse. Do not use every herb in the list above, but you can use as many as you can and bundle those up. You can burn these herbs around you. Use a piece of string or twine to bundle the herbs together and light them. It is best to do this outside. The curse cast on you will be broken when the herb bundle burns away.

Since vetiver, wormwood and mugwort are powerful herbs, they can be used to break any curse or ward off bad spirits. You should carry these herbs with you if you want to protect yourself from any future hex or curse. Fill a small pouch and carry these herbs with you. Leave this bag in your pocket or tie it around your waist.

## Using Positive Energy

**Using Laughter to Break the Curse, Hex, or Spell**

It is important to understand that any dark spell or curse only becomes more powerful because of your negative energy. Therefore, you need to be positive to weaken the spell. Laughter is the best way to rid yourself of the spell or lessen the strength of the curse. You can use it to weaken any type of curse and you do not need any spell or ritual to do this. You only need to be positive.

If you feel the effects of a curse, focus on something funny and happy, and this will make you laugh. Watch a funny video, read a book, or watch a movie. You can enjoy yourself fully. If you find yourself in front of the person who cursed you, be friendly and smile at them. Laugh at something or crack a joke. The person may not find the joke funny, but his power to cause harm to you will weaken.

**Use a Binding Spell**

You can use a binding spell from the earlier chapter to change negative or evil energy to good. This is white or positive magic, and the spell you cast will make it easier to change negative to positive energy. This would mean the person couldn't harm you with any more hexes or curses. Binding spells do not harm anybody. These spells only prevent the person from causing you any more harm. If you want to use a binding spell, write the person's name on a candle and burn the candle. You can repeat the following words:

*"I bring you forth from the dark and hold you to the light. Let not your past control my present. Let not my future be as dark as night. I meet and greet you with open arms and move you back into the light. So, mote it be."*

**Talk to a Healer**

If you believe someone has cast a very strong spell on you, you should meet with a spiritual healer. This person can remove the hex or curse by performing different rituals and remove the curse. You can also speak to someone who knows what you are going through. He can help you identify how to remove this curse so you progress through life.

- Talk to a religious leader if you are religious and looking for some guidance

- Speak to a psychic if you need to. Ensure you speak to someone who is authentic and knows how to work with spells

- You can also speak to a therapist who is open about healing techniques such as hypnosis, meditation, and other unconventional methods to add more positive energy

# Chapter Fourteen

# Principles Used to
# Distinguish Different Types of Spells

Any spell is successful if it is cast with a purpose or intent behind it. In simple words, any spell you choose to cast should be in response to a burning need or desire. It could be something as simple as protecting yourself. You can cast the spell based on a certain event or an idea. Do not perform any spells when you are under emotional stress or duress. The outcome of any spell you cast will reflect how you feel when you cast the spell. If you are going to cast the spell in a crazy or emotional situation, expect grave results. If you want to create meaningful or positive outcomes, focus on your energy and the spell you want to cast.

## Learn to Channel Your Energy with Empathy, Focus, and Wisdom

Every spell you cast is an intermediary, which can unify the different entities you are calling out to through various concepts. There are numerous ways for one to create a spell since there are different types of spells. Each of these spells binds or unites entities in different ways. These patterns show how you can create a spell to create or break any bond. When you choose to create a spell, you must consider the following attributes:

## Correspondences

A correspondence is a link between the physical and intangible. You can form this bond using different tools used to create spells. The time you choose to cast the spell also determines the strength of the link. For example, when you cast a spell, you focus on different planets, and each planet is connected to a distinctive action or concept. Mars is symbolic of determination, while Venus represents romance. In the same way, every other celestial body discovered and used in magic is associated with different days of the week. If you want to cast a protection spell, cast it on Thursday. If you want to cast a love spell, choose Friday.

Most of these links or correspondences have been used for years. There are some correspondences identified recently that are used very often in magic and spell casting. For example, a mirror is often used in incantations or spells as a vessel. Numerous connections have been made so ensure that you look for a bond or correspondence matching the desired outcome of interest.

## Antipathy and Sympathy

Antipathy is the phenomenon where you use repelling forces, while sympathy is one where you use a force to attract another. The latter is based on the assumption that two entities or objects can be joined in one realm and they will be united in other realms. In simple words, this type of magic believes in the concept of the law of attraction, where like attracts like. Any spell using sympathy as its base uses the movement of candles close to each other. A union can be formed by joining the two candles, and you can bind the candles using honeysuckle. This will indicate you are ready to or have already started a relationship or partnership with the person. This is a type of spell you can use to ward off the negative energy from bullies and build effective relationships with them.

You can use this attribute in binding spells. You need to say your intention loudly and be confident about it. Once you have stated your intention, you can light the candle and let it burn completely. If you do not think it is safe for you to let the candle burn throughout the day, you can state your intent or the spell every time you light the candle. Observe the flame when you light the candle:

1.  Is the flame moving erratically?

2.  Has the light begun to dim?

3.  Is the flame robust?

The flame is an indication of how robust your intention is. Once the candle completely burns, the spell you have cast is complete.

As mentioned earlier, antipathy is an attribute in a spell used to repel energy. If you want to remove something from your life, bind a candle tightly with a wire or twine. Put this candle in the freezer and leave it on the ice. You can also write the person's name on an envelope or paper and drop it in the mailbox. Do not write a written address. Let the paper go places.

## Contagion

If you gift a special charm to someone you love, it will determine the closeness of the relationship between you and the person you are gifting the charm to share. This charm will begin to represent your connection with the other person. Any contagion spell is based on the concept that once you contact the person, you are going to be in touch with them. This indicates you will be in touch with everybody you give a charm to despite where you both are.

If you want to perform a contagion spell, you need to find something belonging to the entity. This can be anything from a piece of clothing to a used pen. There is a link between the object and entity. Therefore, any intent you put out there through your spell will magnify.

## Inversion

Use inversion spells if you think you have been impacted by a jinx, psychic attack, or some bad energy. An inversion spell will stimulate certain immunities. An inversion spell is synonymous with a vaccine. In the latter, a small dose of the toxin is pushed into your body to build strength by producing antibodies. Enchanted mirrors and evil eye talismans are used to reflect any ill wishes on the people around you. You can also use cayenne pepper if you want to remove any antagonistic energy from the environment.

## Repetition

A magical connection is often formed or strengthened through regular spell casting. These connections can help you focus on your intent. Creating a rhythm helps to build the energy needed to charge the spell. If you write your crush's name repeatedly and recite a chant, you can strengthen the bond between the two of you. It becomes easy to create a link between magical and physical energy through spells.

# Conclusion

There are two types of magic – white and black magic. White magic is what you should use to protect yourself and your loved ones. Any form of magic uses the concept of manifestation. It also is based on the concept of attracting like. Therefore, your intent and the energy you put out into the universe are what you will attract. Most people worry that this practice is based on lies since quite a few people out there do not believe in magic or witchcraft.

Most white magic spells focus only on the use of good intentions. This indicates white magic is harmless and pure. This book sheds some light on the different forms of magic and helps you learn more about how you can cast spells. It also teaches you about how you can use magic to protect yourself and your loved ones. As a beginner, you may have many questions about the rules and culture. This book provides all the information you need about spell casting.

Any form of magic is only as strong as the spellcaster's intent, and if you want to cast the right spells and manifest your intent in the world, use the energy within yourself and in the objects on your altar to intensify the intent. This book has helped you explore how you can protect yourself and your loved ones using different ingredients and amulets or other protective enchantments.

Since you can use different objects as protection charms, you can use crystals and herbs to intensify or enhance their intent. If you are a beginner, use this book as your guide. It has all the information you need about spell casting and helps you cast the right spells with no negative effects on you. Do not worry about making mistakes, as you can learn from them.

Thank you for buying and reading/listening to our book. If you found this book useful/helpful please take a few minutes and leave a review on Amazon.com or Audible.com (if you bought the audio version).

# References

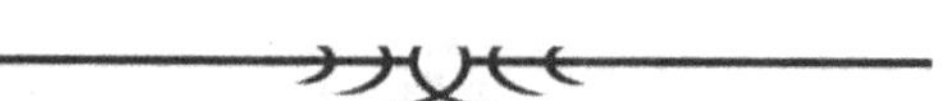


Caro, T. (2019). 5 Free Protection Spells For Loved Ones [Protection Magic]. Magickalspot.com. https://magickalspot.com/protection-spells-guide/

G, B. (2021, April 14). What Is a Binding Spell? When and How to Use It Safely. Exemplore. https://exemplore.com/wicca-witchcraft/How-and-When-to-Use-a-Binding-Spell

Faragher, A. K. (2018, March 26). A Beginner's Guide to Casting Your Own Spells. Allure. https://www.allure.com/story/how-to-cast-spells

Jones, R. (2019, September 20). The Sims 4 Spellcasters guide: How to become a Spellcaster in the Realm of Magic expansion. Eurogamer. https://www.eurogamer.net/articles/2019-09-13-the-sims-4-spellcaster-realm-of-magic-6026

Magic Spells Guide for Beginners (9 Safety Tips to Know). (2020, November 16). SF Weekly. https://www.sfweekly.com/sponsored/magic-spells-guide-for-beginners-9-safety-tips-to-know/

May, A. (n.d.). Powerful Protection Spells For Beginner Witches. Welcome to Wicca Now. https://wiccanow.com/powerful-protection-spells-for-beginner-witches/

Remove Black Magic Spells. (2011, January 27). WikiHow;
     wikiHow. https://www.wikihow.com/Remove-Black-Magic-
     Spells

Telesco, P. (2018, April 24). Ten Tips for Casting Successful
     Magic Spells. Wise Witches and Witchcraft.
     https://witchcraftandwitches.com/spells/ten-tips-for-casting-
     successful-magic-spells/

Thomson, D. (2018, July 24). 5 Ways To Use Binding Spells To
     Protect Your Love From Harm. Pandagossips.com.
     https://pandagossips.com/posts/1732

Whitehurst, T. (2021, February 23). 5 Spells to Protect Yourself
     from Challenging People. Tess Whitehurst.
     https://tesswhitehurst.com/5-spells-to-protect-yourself-from-
     challenging-people